YOUR HEROES, MY GRANDPARENTS

YOUR HEROES, MY GRANDPARENTS

A GRANDDAUGHTER'S LOVE

By Julie Rogers Pomilia

BRITON

810 Eastgate North Dr., Suite 200
Cincinnati, Ohio 45245
www.britonpublishing.com

ISBN 978-1-956216-09-7 Hardcover
ISBN 978-1-956216-11-0 Paperback

Briton Publishing, LLC books are distributed by Ingram Content Group and made available worldwide.

Briton Publishing would like to make a note that most of the photos in this book were taken before the digital age of photography that we now know and have become accustomed to. Therefore, the quality may not be up to the standard we normally see in our books. That said, we felt that each of these photos not only carry special memories and stories for the author and readers, many of them have never been seen before by the public and provide an intimate look into Roy and Dale's private life. We would like to thank the reader for being understanding and enjoying these photos and the memories associated with them.

This book is dedicated to Taylor, Trevor, and Brendan who have come a long way from doing the limbo under the rope in the bank line, scrambling to be first to press the elevator button, and keeping that dead snake you named Steven in the freezer for 12 years. What an adventure. It is the joy of my life to be your mom, and watch you grow into the wonderful men that you are. Within these pages you will find short stories ... not a full meal, but a snack of your family heritage. Since you three were my initial inspiration in writing these memories, there's a decent chance you'll be getting this book for Christmas ... even if it's not on your list. Oh, and remember, having a weird mom builds character. You're welcome!

ACKNOWLEDGMEMTS

Thank you, Gino, for encouraging me to keep writing, and for your unwavering love and support, among the 1,000 other things you do. You're the best!

To Brinka, my editor, my lifelong friend, and the only person I've ever met who came into this world on exactly the same day, and same year as me. I'm pretty sure that we were twins separated at birth. No wonder we work so well together! My heartfelt thanks.

TABLE OF CONTENTS

To My Niece, Cabbage

You know, I'm not even sure when or why I started calling you that. Somewhere along the way, it fit your personality and just sort of stuck. You are quirky, but very sweet and lovable ... definitely the most like your grandmother of anyone in our family.

We don't often realize the full value of people in our lives until they become a memory. So, I'm glad that you have written this book. You had a very unique relationship with them, which was one-of-a-kind. These are your experiences, and yours alone. I hope those who read these stories appreciate where your words are coming from — the heart. I also hope your sons cherish this memoir of a very special lady they call Mom.

I'm proud of you.

Roy Rogers Jr.
(Uncle Dustbowl)

FOREWORD

by
ROB WORD

How exciting to know that your grandparents were the King and Queen of Western Movies. Roy Rogers and Dale Evans were that husband-and-wife team. This is the storybook tale of a little girl who had a royal pair of relatives and cherished every moment. Better yet, she remembered those years and has written about those special times that shed a warm, loving light on her legendary grandparents in stories untold ... until now.

Julie Rogers Pomilia was that little girl with very special celebrity grandparents. Her father was Tom Fox, Dale Evans' only biological son from her first marriage. Roy and Dale married in 1947. Julie's "Grampy" and Grandma were household names, known around the world. They starred together in hugely popular musical Westerns at Republic Pictures, co-starred in a family-friendly TV series, co-hosted dozens of television network and syndicated variety shows, headlined rodeos, sold millions of records, and had their own radio series. Did that leave the two aging icons much time for their expanding brood? They made time! For them, family came first.

Julie's stories about her grandparents shed light on their generosity, their struggles, and how these two ordinary folks set examples for several generations representing truth, justice, and, yes, the American way. Their unforgettable theme song was "Happy Trails to You," written by Dale, who also penned the Sunday School classic, "The Bible Tells Me So."

As a longtime fan and friend of Roy and Dale, my wife and I were at their 50th wedding anniversary celebration. We were thrilled to be included and to share that momentous occasion with them, their family, and friends. I first met Roy in 1972 in Orlando, Florida, and invited him to be a guest on "Night Owl Theater," my late-night movie series, to talk about his Westerns. He agreed, we discussed, and then showed *Dark Command*, one of his few non-B-Western starring roles. Heck, he co-starred with John Wayne in the large-scale production and played Claire

Trevor's impetuous younger brother! Roy was so charming and kind to a young film buff. He was exactly what all those of us in my generation expected. When Roy came back through town later, both he and Dale appeared with me on the show, which is still a very special memory.

I am honored to be asked to write the foreword for Julie's book. She seems to be at every Western film festival and tribute to her famous grandparents and brightens up every room she enters. She's got lots of fans, too, and her book should be an instant smash for all of them. One nice thing about writing the foreword is that it gave me an opportunity to read in advance the delicious stories she shares. Julie takes us all inside the cavernous ranch house and into numerous nooks and crannies where she discovered stacks of merchandise, toys, Roy Rogers Comics, and closets full of those fancy glittering rhinestone outfits Roy and Dale wore for personal appearances. As an inquisitive little wrangler, Julie remembers their friend Nudie, who designed those outrageous western costumes and spotting the now rare lapel of an actual nude cowgirl.

These pages, written with love and tender care by Julie, will have you wanting more. I know I did! Find out what it was like for a little girl to discover that her fun-loving Grampy was known all over the world. Was our hero Roy as much fun at home as all of us fans hoped he would be? Family gatherings were huge at the Rogers' ranch, and they happened often. There were numerous aunts, uncles, cousins, and nephews that filled her weekends at the ranch.

Did Roy really love kids and animals? You bet. He adored them. Julie takes us on early trips to the barn to see Trigger, "the Smartest Horse in the Movies," and reveals how many different horses were used in the making of the B-Western classics. What sort of personality did "The Old Man," the original Trigger, have? How about Dale's horse, Buttermilk? Not the same personality at all!

With so many mouths to feed, was there enough room for everyone? Was there enough food? What was the pecking order? Julie answers these questions with a delightfully charming sense of humor. What fun they had. Reading this book is almost like being a part of the family.

Julie takes you down many paths to celebrate her grandparent's amazing life and legacy and she does it with love, humor, pride, and a sense of history as only an insider could deliver. This book is filled with gems; memories of generosity, world-famous celebrities, family gatherings at Christmas, and the many, many birthdays to celebrate. Even though there was much fun and many games as Julie was growing up, her story is not all laughter. There is sorrow and tragedy, too.

If you know anything about Roy and Dale, love family fun, and cherish friends and heroes, this book, that you are holding in your hands right now, will be very hard to put down.

Rob Word is a veteran television executive and producer and a founding father of the Golden Boot Awards. Word's love of the genre includes hosting and producing A WORD ON WESTERNS, his long-running celebrity interview series on YouTube, and executive producer for the 1995 documentary "Roy Rogers: An American Hero" for A & E's biography series.

Chapter 1:

WHO WERE ROY ROGERS AND DALE EVANS?

Roy Rogers was born Leonard Franklin Slye, in Cincinnati, Ohio on November 5, 1911. He was an American actor, singer, and television host, fondly known as the King of the Cowboys. But coming from humble beginnings, and being extremely bashful, Leonard never dreamed of becoming an actor. He was going to be a dentist. But in searching for a better life, his mom and dad packed up their family and moved out to California, where he picked peaches along the way and played his guitar to make a little extra cash for the family.

Upon arriving in Los Angeles, his sister, Mary, convinced him to sing in a talent show on the radio. After doing pretty well, he then mustered up the courage to join a band, which was performing regularly. Over the next few years, one thing led to another, Leonard changed his name to Roy, and his first big break as an actor, was in 1938 when he was chosen for the lead role in the movie, *Under Western Stars*, to replace Gene Autry who was in a contract dispute with the studio. Then this unlikely movie star went on to become the number one Western box office star for eleven straight years in a row, from 1943 to 1954. Under contract with Republic Studios, Roy made more than 100 films, and as many as six films a year, seen annually by over 80 million Americans. A whole generation of children spent their Saturday afternoons at the neighborhood matinee theater, watching the adventures of Roy Rogers and his golden palomino horse, Trigger. As a matter of fact, in the 1940s, *Life* Magazine conducted a poll for children, and posed the question, *Who would you most want to be like?* It was a three-way tie between President Franklin D. Roosevelt, Abraham Lincoln, and Roy Rogers.

Roy Rogers married his frequent co-star, Dale Evans, in 1947, and they went on to star together in the popular TV Western, *The Roy Rogers Show*, which ran for nine years on radio before moving to television, airing on NBC for six seasons from 1951 to 1957.

During the 1950s, the Roy Rogers Fan Club had nearly 2.5 million members in the U.S. and 90,000 members in England, which had been the biggest fan club before the Beatles came along. He felt that he owed it to his loyal fans to respond to each letter personally. But on his salary of $75 a week at Republic, he could not even keep up with the cost of buying the stamps he needed in order to answer the 79,000 fan letters he received in just one month. When he asked for help from the studio his boss, Herbert Yates, he suggested he just throw the fan mail away like some of the other stars did. Roy wouldn't do that.

As a result, he began working summers, traveling around the country to perform at State Fairs and rodeos with his family. He also made extra cash from selling Roy Rogers merchandise.

But the amount of fan mail grew as Roy's repeated requests for help fell on deaf ears. He finally rented a 5-ton dump truck and filled it with his fan mail. He then drove over to the studio and backed the truck up on the lawn in front of Herbert Yates' office, dumping the mail in front of him to prove his point. Roy then drove away, glancing in his rearview mirror to see Yates wildly gesturing in a combustible tirade. The outcome? He received a small raise. That's the upstanding person Roy Rogers was.

He was one of the most popular Western movie stars during the era of the singing cowboys. The B-Westerns were often regarded as the bottom of the Western movie food chain because these low-budget films had predictable plots, mediocre acting, and usually appealed to younger audiences. But the truth is, these films were an important part of Western movie history, and also served as the means to provide financial stability for the studio to make the higher-profile big-budget films each year.

Roy is the only performer to have been inducted twice into the Country Music Hall of Fame, once as a part of the Sons of the Pioneers, and the second time as an individual performer. Out of the 2700 celebrities who have a star on Hollywood's Walk of Fame, Roy Rogers, along with Bob Hope, Mickey Rooney, and Tony Martin are the only performers who have, not just one, but four stars, with each star recognizing accomplishments in radio, music, film, and television.

Dale Evans was an actress, considered to be the most popular woman ever to appear in Western movies. Riding her horse, Buttermilk, and singing alongside Roy Rogers, she was appropriately dubbed, "The Queen of the West." Dale was born Frances Octavia Smith, in Uvalde, Texas, on October 31, 1912. She dreamed very early on of becoming a glamorous star.

Unlike Roy, she struggled to work her way into show biz by singing evenings for a local radio program, while working as a stenographer by day. She sang jazz, swing, and big band music, aspiring to someday be cast in big, extravagant musicals. Dale encountered much heartache along the way through job rejections, and failed marriages, with one of which, she had a son.

Her momentum as a singer finally began to pick up when she was chosen as the featured singer on the Edgar Bergen/Charlie McCarthy radio show, which paved the way for a screen test and a contract with 20th Century Fox. She did a few romantic comedies, which never got much attention. Certainly, the last place she ever envisioned herself, was in Westerns. But she did, in fact, screen test at Republic Studios with the rising young Western star, Roy Rogers, and she ended up becoming exactly that, a singing cowgirl.

Dale wrote the theme song, "Happy Trails", for their TV show. Together they starred in 35 films and recorded more than 400 songs. She authored twenty-nine books, and she too, has not one, but two stars on Hollywood's Walk of Fame.

Roy and Dale went on to have 9 children, 16 grandchildren, and more than 30 great-grandchildren. The author, Julie Rogers Pomilia, is the youngest daughter of Tom Fox, Dale's only biological son from her first marriage, who later became one of the siblings in this "yours, mine, and ours" menagerie of the Rogers nine children. What follows in these pages is one granddaughter's recollections, of what life was like growing up with her famous grandparents, the King of Cowboys and the Queen of the West.

Roy Rogers and Dale Evans, fondly known as "The King of the
Cowboys" and "The Queen of the West," starred in 35 films
together, recorded more than 400 songs, and were considered the
most popular western couple during the 1950s.

One week's worth of mail. During a six-month period in 1945, when Roy was the number one box office star, the United States Postal Service documented 422,511 pieces of fan mail addressed to Roy Rogers.

Dale as "Kansas Kate" in the 1945 film. *Sunset in Eldorado*.

She wanted to be in big productions and glamorous musicals,

. . . but became a cowgirl instead.

Chapter 2:

WILL THE "REAL" CHILD PLEASE STAND UP?

"So Roy isn't your real grandfather."

"Wait, you're not really related to Dale then, are you?"

"Ohhhhhh. So you were one of the adopted ones."

These have always been curious comments to me. All of us have heard it in some form or another, from well-meaning people, which has driven me to ask myself one question. What does "real" even mean? I've concluded that if the criteria for being a "real" child means biological, then I guess millions of adopted children across the globe don't have "real" parents, and to follow that line of thinking, my grandparents had only one child. The only child who could have ever claimed both Roy and Dale as her biological parents would have been little Robin Elizabeth. All of the other eight siblings, including my dad, sadly were never a "real" child of one, or the other, or both. But it gets even worse. If you follow this jolly trolley, that means none of their grandchildren are "real" either. Oh, dear. I'm one of those. Chaos in the streets of Saskatoon. Do we really want to pull this thread? Well, if we are going to get to the bottom of this, and someone has to, then it might as well be me.

We are the quintessential "Yours, Mine, and Ours" family with adopted, foster, and biological origins. The funny thing is, none of us have ever given it much thought, because Grandma and Grandpa never made a distinction between us. There was no pecking order. No Rogers sibling was better than the other, or "more" their child than the rest. The simple fact of the matter is, that we are, and have always been, just family. Roy and Dale had nine children. Yes, you did hear that correctly. Nine. That's a lot of laundry.

I never knew a biological grandfather. My mom's dad had died when she was 16, long before I was born, and her mother had remarried. So the two grandfathers I grew up with on both my mom and dad's side, (Granddaddy Campbell, and Grandpa Roy) were not my biological grandfathers, but they were the only ones I ever knew. Every person in my family has a similar version of this basic story. So you can see how tricky it gets when you use "real" interchangeably with "biological," at least in our family. When I was younger, it was tempting to let people's assumptions be like that stick that wedges in between the spokes of my bike, bringing my concept of a "secure family" to an abrupt halt, sending me flying over the proverbial handlebars. However, now, as an adult, I know that our family is just hard to sort out, and people simply want to get it straight. So when they ask, I'm always happy to explain.

You might still wobble away, scratching your head, but I'll take a stab at it. I've listed the Rogers siblings in chronological order of when they entered the family, and not necessarily by age. But to further assist in untangling this diverse family of ours, I have also listed the Rogers siblings in order from oldest to youngest. Here we go.

Dale actually started it all off when she eloped with her first beau, Thomas Fox when she was 14 years of age. A few months later, at fifteen, she had a son,

THOMAS FOX JR, born in 1927 (DALE'S ONLY BIOLOGICAL SON WITH 1ST HUSBAND).

Young Tom would not only become the oldest of the Rogers siblings but would eventually become my dad. Being career driven, however, she would send Tom (off and on) between the ages of six and thirteen to live with her parents or other relatives. She would also marry and divorce two more times before she would meet her forever love, Roy Rogers.

Now, over in Ohio, when Roy was young, he married a girl named Lucille Ascolese. It lasted three years before divorcing. They had no children. He then married his second wife, Grace Arline Wilkins, in 1936. They thought they were unable to have children, so Roy and Arline adopted a little 6-month-old girl named,

CHERYL in 1941 (ROY'S ONLY ADOPTED DAUGHTER WITH 2ND WIFE, ARLINE).

Then, as it so often happens after adopting, Arline got pregnant, and they saw the birth of their daughter,

LINDA LOU in 1943 (ROY AND ARLINE'S ONLY BIOLOGICAL DAUGHTER).

Finally, Roy and Arline were ecstatic to find out they were going to have a little boy. They named him,

ROY ROGERS, JR. ("Dusty") in 1946 (ROY AND ARLINE'S ONLY BIOLOGICAL SON).

A week later, Arline died of an embolism.

On New Year's Eve of 1947, Roy Rogers (the now single dad to three small children — Cheryl, Linda Lou, and Dusty) married his co-star, Dale Evans (who had the one son, Tom, who was now 21).

Because both Roy and Dale loved children, they wanted to add to their growing family of four. In 1950, Dale gave birth to the only child they would both share biologically,

ROBIN in 1950 (ROY AND DALE'S ONLY BIOLOGICAL DAUGHTER TOGETHER)

Sadly, Robin was born with Down Syndrome and serious heart defects. She only lived for two years. After contracting the mumps from her siblings, and developing complications, she passed two days before her second birthday.

Heartbroken, and still desiring more children, Roy and Dale began noticing the little ones they would see in the children's hospitals and orphanages they visited. They decided to adopt two more children on the same trip,

MARY LITTLE DOE ("Dodie") in 1952 (ADOPTED BY ROY AND DALE) and JOHN DAVID ("Sandy") in 1952 (ADOPTED BY ROY AND DALE)

Dodie was 7-months old, and a Choctaw Native American just like Roy, which made it easier to obtain clearance to adopt her. Sandy was 5 years old. He had been severely abused and then abandoned as a child, sustaining mild brain damage and a broken nose. Their hearts melted, wondering what would happen to a little guy like that, so they brought him home.

Next, they adopted a 12-year-old Scottish girl, while on a rodeo tour in Britain,

MARION ("Mimi") in 1954 (FOSTERED, AND THEN ADOPTED BY ROY AND DALE)

The last to be adopted was a 3-year-old Korean war orphan named,

IN AI LEE (Debbie) in 1955 (THE LAST CHILD ADOPTED BY ROY AND DALE)

This is the last photo taken of who was left of the Rogers siblings in 2008 at Uncle Gary's memorial service (Linda Lou's husband) **Back row:** Dusty, Mimi, Cheryl, and Dodie. **Front row:** Linda Lou and Tom Since this photo was taken, both Tom and Mimi have passed.

IN ORDER BY AGE FROM OLDEST TO YOUNGEST

Tom Fox (Born November 28, 1927, and died at age 84 on May 16, 2012, from congestive heart failure)

Cheryl Barnett Rogers (Born June 6, 1940 – Present)

Marion "Mimi" (Born December 19, 1940, and died at age 80 on January 25, 2021, from a brain aneurysm)

Linda Lou (Born 1943 – Present)

Roy Jr. "Dusty" (Born October 28, 1946 – Present)

John David "Sandy" (Born June 17, 1947, and died at age 18 on October 30, 1965 from an unfortunate accident while in Germany)

Robin (Born August 26, 1950, and died at 23 months on August 24, 1952, due to complications from the mumps)

Mary Little Doe "Dodie" (Born on March 19, 1952 – Present)

Debbie (Born in Korea on August 14, 1952, and died at age 12 on August 17, 1964, in a bus crash)

This is our wonderfully diverse, multi-cultural family in a nutshell. Obviously, that was just the beginning and dozens more have been added to the family tree. My Aunt Dodie and I often do western festivals together, having way more fun than two people ought to have. We look nothing alike, but we do think alike, which is quite scary for our husbands. We work well as a team.

I love my relatives. I feel very blessed to have been born into such a unique family where, from the top down, integrity and kindness were consistently modeled. So, embrace your family, because whether biological or not, they are still your family.

Tom Fox (my dad) as a toddler.

Little Robin dancing with Dale.

The Rogers with the other seven children.

Two decades later, Grandma Dale gave me the outfit she is wearing in the photo above. Why? I'm not really sure, but she really seemed to love passing clothes on to me. She liked this outfit so much that she had two jackets made for it. I am wearing the skirt with the second matching jacket.

This was me sitting on my grandfather's lap (on my mother's side) "Real" or "step" never made any difference, they were all real to each of us.

Chapter 3:

I'D LIKE A GRAMPY PLEASE

If you've ever ordered a "Shirley Temple" off of a drink menu, you know that it's made with ginger ale and a splash of grenadine, topped with a maraschino cherry. Created when Shirley Temple was around 10 years old in the 1930s, the drink came to represent the wholesomeness she portrayed, and also provided kids with a non-alcoholic substitute when out to dinner with adults. Chances are, if you know about the "Shirley Temple," you probably know what a "Roy Rogers," is too. It's basically the boy's version of a Shirley Temple, but it's made with Coca-Cola instead of ginger ale.

I have sipped my share of Roy Rogers drinks over the years, which is, in itself, nothing particularly notable. I guess the oddity of it for me, (and my 15 other cousins), is that this drink is not only named after a good guy in a white hat, but it is named after someone I call Grandpa.

We sat in a little Mexican restaurant in Auburn, California with our first son, Taylor, who was 4 years old. I happened to notice that they had Shirley Temples and Roy Rogers drinks on the menu. I leaned over to my son, and said to him, "You know, there's a drink here named after Grampy." Taylor sat up straight. "Really, can I have one?" he asked. "Sure!" I answered. The server came back to our table, and Taylor very sensibly said, "I'd like a Grampy please." Coaching him quietly, I whispered, "Um ... you have to actually say his name." Needless to say, we had to iron out a few details on that one before our next dinner out.

As I think back on that dinner, Taylor was undoubtedly very pleased, but not overly impressed by the fact that his drink was named after his great-grandpa. That's sort of how I grew up. There was never any arrogance or entitlement. It was just the way it was. This is, in fact, how all of my memories are of my extraordinary grandparents. I say, "extraordinary," not because of what they did, but because of the kind of people they were. You knew them as the King of the Cowboys and the Queen of the West. I knew them as simply, "Grandma and Grandpa."

"Gigi and Grampy" spontaneously visited Taylor at his preschool on "Cowboy Day." His little friends hardly noticed, but his teachers nearly fainted.

Photo by David Valdez

Clint Black and Roy Rogers sing their Grammy nominated song, "Hold on Partner", at the 25th anniversary of the CMA Awards held at the Grand Ole Opry House on October 1, 1991 in Nashville, Tennessee. Among those in the audience was President George H.W. Bush who was sitting in the second row.

Roy and Dale on the Red Carpet in 1992 for the 34th Grammy Awards, Radio City Music Hall, New York City.

Chapter 4:

WHO'S ON THE COVER?

People have always asked me, "Wasn't it weird growing up with famous grandparents?" That's a puzzling thought for me because "normal" is whatever you grow up with. You never think something is weird or different if that's all you know.

My grandparents lived most of their lives in the public's view, and they accepted that as part of the package. Meanwhile, the rest of the family lived on the edge of that spotlight, enjoying anonymity. When we did go out in public with them, we would sample small doses of what they experienced every day. So I got used to people following us, staring, pointing, and whispering. We grew accustomed to waiting patiently while out for dinner, as random people would approach our table wanting their autographs or a photo. One time, I did get a bit swept off to the side by a small wave of people, who began pressing in to meet them, as we were all coming out of a theater where they had just finished a performance. That startled me, and I squealed, "Hey! Don't leave me!" Art Rush, their manager, simply stepped through the crowd and grabbed my hand, helping me back to the car.

At the ranch, sometimes we would sit on the floor and watch "The Roy Rogers Show" with Grandpa. "Come on Roy. Go get 'em, Roy! Get those bad guys!" he would hoot with a silly grin. We thought nothing of that. It was just fun. For all I knew, everybody's grandpa had a TV show. They floated seamlessly back and forth from their roles as Grandma and Grandpa to Roy and Dale. They could put on their make-up in their bedroom in Chatsworth, and then step out into the 300 acres they owned behind their ranch to film a western scene, among all of those dirt roads, huge rocks, and sagebrush. It all seemed very natural to me. This was my normal, and it was only when I began noticing other people's reactions that I questioned it.

When I was young, I attended a private school called Pasadena Christian School in Southern California. I always loved "Back-to-School" shopping with my mom, getting new black and white saddle shoes, a few new dresses, and above all, the smell of a brand-new box of crayons with those colorful, pointed tips sitting all neatly in a row when I opened the box for the first time. I had a crazy, overactive imagination, and wouldn't you know, on the first day of kindergarten, I met my little bestie, Diane, who was very eager to do the same kinds of things. We would bring small magnets to school inside a tiny cardboard box. Then, under the Eucalyptus tree in the play yard, we would pan for gold like miners, dragging the magnets around, lifting those mysterious iron filings out of the dirt. We would place our treasure in the box and bury it back under the tree, marking the dirt above it with a secret pebble or stick. The next recess, we would then be pirates, looking for gold, and we would dig our secret treasure back up. Diane and I have remained friends after all of these years, and amazingly enough, we both remember these experiences together with detail and fondness.

I believe that my imagination and creativity was profoundly influenced by both of my grandmothers. My mom's mother, being a kindergarten teacher, encouraged imaginative play. My Grandma Mabel would push me on her swing in her backyard, and recite poems to me, and tell me fantastic stories. Then we would pretend that I was flying off to an imaginary land, riding on one of the desert tortoises she actually had in her backyard, which was legal back then. While I pumped back and forth on the swing, I would close my eyes and describe my jaunty trip up through the clouds made of cotton candy. Sometimes she would bring over to my house, a simple cardboard box, and together we would transform it into some crazy imaginary animal. Other times, she would put a box of bright, silk scarves down on the living room floor. Then she would play the piano and I would dance around the living room to the music making grand swipes through the air with the colors. Over on the other side of the San Fernando Valley, I would see my Grandma Dale of course on their television show, pretending to serve breakfast at a diner, or riding out alongside Roy to catch some diamond thieves. She and Grandpa were always dressing up in costumes, so I was immersed on all sides with colorful fancies and imagination.

While at school, we regularly received those newsprint booklets from Scholastic News, called "Weekly Readers," which our teachers would pass out to each student, and then read together. One day, as my class was quietly working, I looked up and noticed my second-grade teacher sitting at her desk, looking at me and smiling. That was curious, I thought. She silently motioned me with her finger to come to see her, so I got out of my seat. When I got to her desk, I noticed a stack of crisp, new Weekly Readers sitting in front of her. She looked down and pointed to the front cover. There, covering the whole front page, was a black-and-white picture of Grandpa on his horse, who was kneeling in the center of a big arena. My teacher pointed to the picture, and whispered, "Do you know who this is?" I answered respectfully, "Yes, that's my grandpa." But in my 7-year-old mind, I was wondering, "Why are you asking me that?"

That day, seeing my teacher's excited reaction, made me start to wonder if maybe my family was different from everyone else's family. I went home that day with a lot of questions, starting off with, "How did my teacher seem to know, or even care, who my grandfather was?" This was the small beginning of understanding their fame and impact on others.

Grandma and Grandpa never assumed they were more important than anyone else. They also never forgot their humble beginnings. In private, they were what all of their fans hoped they would be — honest, loyal, and kind. They were endearingly funny, and they would give you the shirt off their back, literally. In fact, years before, a fan complimented Grandma on her vest. Right then and there, Grandma took it off and gave it to the woman. That vest is now proudly displayed in a tiny museum just outside Portsmouth, Ohio. The only problem is that I have the other half of that outfit hanging in my closet to wear for western events. I guess it will just have to be like one of those Mizpah friendship coin necklaces where each person owns one half.

You and I both had screen time with them. The only difference? You saw them on the big screen, and I saw them through the screen door while asking for a popsicle. They loved God, family, and their country, and having spent so much time with them while growing up, they helped shape me into the person I have become as an adult. For that, and so much more, I am deeply grateful.

Even today, some fifty years later, whenever I see that particular photo of Grandpa and his horse, it takes me all the way back to standing beside my second-grade teacher at her desk. I am 7 years old again. I am curious, and I am smiling.

Me in second grade.

This was the photo of Grandpa on the cover of the Weekly Reader that
day in second grade.

The vest is at the little museum outside of Portsmouth, OH, and it's matching split skirt is in my closet at home.

Chapter 5:

FRIDAY NIGHTS AT THE RANCH

The ranch in Chatsworth was magical to me. My family lived in Montrose, a little town nestled in the foothills of the San Gabriel Mountains, between Glendale and Pasadena, California. I always looked forward to the weekends, when my parents, my sisters, and I would pile into our old yellow station wagon and drive out to the San Fernando Valley to Grandma and Grandpa's ranch, about 20 minutes away. They had bought 300 acres in Chatsworth that backed up to Iverson Movie Ranch where they filmed a lot of their Westerns.

"Are we there yet?" I would ask. Finally, I would feel the tires rumble onto the little bumpy road leading up to the house, and I knew we were close. I could hardly sit still, giddy with excitement, as we wound slowly around the base of the foothills to their ranch. Shortly before reaching the house, we would soon be passing the barn on the left where the horses were. "Ok, let's guess! Will Trigger be inside or outside the barn?" I would hold my breath with anticipation as we rounded the corner. Yessss! There he was, his beautiful golden coat, reflecting the last few rays of sunlight. I never tired of that sight, as I stretched my neck out the car window for one last glimpse, before disappearing around the next curve.

As we neared the actual driveway, I could now see the sprawling ranch house with the red-tiled roof. By this time, I could hear the dogs barking. I knew in a moment, that they would be dashing out to run alongside our car, as we rolled to a stop in front of the carport. That was where Nellybelle, the gray Jeep from their TV show was often parked. Then just like clockwork, Grandma would step out the back Dutch door calling, "Woo Hoo! Woo Hoo!" drying her hands on her apron. I'd bust out of the car, and run to her outstretched arms. "Hi, Sugarfoot!" she would exclaim as she hugged me. I would close my eyes in her embrace and grin with delight. The weekend was here! And so it began every time.

Inside the house, the familiar smell of Grandma's lemon garlic salad permeated the air. Dinner was cooking in the pot and the aroma of rolls browning in the oven brought me instant comfort. The boisterous chatter of the adults, kids, and dogs running around, made for the happy chaos I had come to feel secure with. I felt safe at this ranch, and my world was wonderful. The table was being set for all of the adults and teenagers who were allowed to sit at the big round table with the gigantic wooden turning platter in the middle that Grandma called Lazy Susan. I always wondered who Susan was, and why Grandma thought she was lazy. Susan enthralled me, and so as aunts and uncles were busy milling around before dinner, and my cousins were scattered, running here and there, I would casually walk over to the big table, pick up a fork next to someone's plate, and place it on Susan, spinning her ever so slowly, careful not to draw attention, until that fork would come around again, stopping right in front of me. This was my routine. I would do this several times with various utensils until someone would finally tell me to go wash up for dinner.

My cousins and I were never allowed to eat at that big table. It was adults only, which actually included my two sisters, Candie and Mindy, who were six and eight years older than me. They were the same age as Dodie and Debbie, my youngest aunts. But I did look forward to eating at the kid's table in the kitchen with my own kind. Laurie, Lisa, Kimmie, Brian, David, Danny, and I, all crowded around the silver-edged soda fountain table with the ivory, leather-like chairs stacked with various heights of phone books for us to sit on. Then the fun would begin. Once we had been served, the adults became so engrossed in their conversation at the big table, they never noticed the chaotic little dinner party going on in the kitchen. The dogs would hover under our feet, and I soon discovered that I could easily feed them anything I didn't like on my plate, which was usually the stew. The dreaded stew.

I didn't really understand why fish had to be on Friday, but I kept seeing it on my plate every weekend. Grandma would add random pieces of other animal meat from Grandpa's hunting trips into that stew, and as it bubbled on the stove, there was no telling what was in that pot. Sometimes elk, sometimes bear, maybe a possum or two. I tried not to think about it, but I always hoped the portion the adult served me would be minimal. It always seemed that no matter how much of that stuff ended up on my plate, the juice would flow around contaminating everything else in its way. I learned to quickly snatch up my roll, and shove the salad and Jell-O up around the edges, trying to make barriers with my napkin to soak up the juice, which, of course, was always a dismal failure, especially for the Jell-O, which usually melted into a puddle of green juice.

Every once in a while, to my dismay, the dogs wouldn't even eat some of the gristly chunks of stew I dropped under the table, leaving me to crawl under and scoop it up with my napkin to throw down the garbage disposal. "I thought you were going to help me," I'd mutter to the dogs under my breath. I survived Grandma's Friday night family dinners on Jell-O, rolls, and salad. This was my world, and I loved it, in spite of the stew.

Exterior of the house on the Chatsworth Ranch.

Nellybelle (the Jeep), Grandpa and Grandma at the entrance of
Chatsworth Ranch.

Grandpa and Grandma sitting above the house in Chatsworth.

Friday night dinner at the adult's table.

Friday night dinner at the kid's table.

Years later, when all of the Rogers' family items were displayed in the museum, I finally made it to the coveted spot at the adult's table with "Lazy Susan." Nothing short of a triumphant moment.

Chapter 6:

MY HAPPY PLACE

One thing I loved more than anything else at Grandma and Grandpa's ranch, was playing in their master bedroom. Our grandparents' massive bedroom at the Chatsworth Ranch was at the end of a long hallway, which I was pretty sure was the longest hallway in the world. It had three doors off the right-hand side. Behind two of the doors, were his and hers closets filled with Grandma and Grandpa's show costumes hanging neatly in a row. I was always drawn into these closets by the intoxicating smell of leather and liniment, with a hint of cologne. I would close my eyes and breathe in deeply. It was enchanting, and all of the bright-colored costumes captivated me. Occasionally, I would stick my scrawny little arm inside one of the bejeweled sleeves and wave it around. If the light was just right, the rhinestones created rainbows of colors that danced on the ceiling. Every shirt had a different design: stars, horses, cactus, flowers, or hearts. Each one seemed more beautiful than the last. I was spellbound by this secret place, but then the moment would quickly pass. Coming to my senses, of being alone, or worse yet, of being found poking around their closets, I would go running out and back up the hallway into the living room.

I didn't know it then, but later as an adult, I would not only end up preserving two of Grandpa's shirts in my own closet, but I would also find out the history of those costumes. A gentleman named, Nudie Cohn, made most of those rhinestone outfits in my grandparents' closet. He was nicknamed "Nudie" because his Russian name was actually, "Nutya Kotlyrenko." However, it was also an ironic nickname because he started his career making costumes for showgirls and strippers back in New York City.

He and his wife, Bobbie, relocated to Los Angeles in the 1940s and expanded their business by making iconic, one-of-a-kind stage costumes for western musicians, outrageously embellished with rhinestones and embroidery. His motto was, " ... the costume is the first impression and it should be flashy." In 1950, he opened his storefront, "Nudie's Rodeo Tailors" in North Hollywood, where he began building his celebrity clientele, outfitting major stars like John Lennon, Sonny and Cher, Aretha Franklin, Elton John, Dolly Parton, Elvis, and of course, Roy and Dale.

His custom-made suits bore labels with an image of a topless cowgirl. In 1963, when Grandma was having an outfit tailored by Nudie, she and Nudie's wife, Bobbie, decided to start dressing the naked cowgirl on the tag with a bolero, for the costumes Grandma wore, in keeping with her conservative image. Now, I'm not really sure who they thought was going to be reaching down Grandma's neck to pull out her tag and check for a topless lady, but nonetheless, they changed it. Consequently, at some point down the road, the tag was permanently changed on all of the clothes Nudie made. Today, the Nudie shirts bearing the topless cowgirl, are actually more valuable and sought after, because there are so few of them left. I'm sure it has nothing to do with the fact that there's a naked lady on the tag. Just saying.

Early on, it was Grandpa's intent to enhance the rodeo experience for every child, even the ones who didn't have the money to sit down close to the arena when he would perform at huge venues like Madison Square Garden. Some had to sit so high up, that they could hardly see Grandma and Grandpa in the center of the ring. So Grandpa asked Nudie to cover his suits with rhinestones from top to bottom so that when the spotlight would hit him, those less fortunate children could see him better. I guess you might say, he was one of, if not the first, "Rhinestone Cowboy." Today, Nudie's granddaughter, Jamie, is a friend of mine, and we have done some western festivals together. Who would have known?

Well, getting back to their master bedroom, Grandpa was really just a big kid who loved gadgets. The master bathroom was done completely in that era's evocative pink tile, and they had one of those 1950s vibrating belt exercise machines, the kind where you stood on a platform that had a wide belt attached to the front column. You'd put that belt around your thighs, turn on the machine and just stand there while the belt supposedly wiggled and jiggled the fat right off you. We'd all take turns on that thing, as the others would giggle while the one on the machine tried to talk. Of course, it always sounded like a buzzing robot voice, like putting your face in front of a fan and talking.

There was also another contraption in their bathroom that frightened me. It was a portable sauna. You'd get inside and sit down on a ledge, closing the door so just your head was sticking out of the neck hole on the top. Then you'd turn up the heat and steam would begin to well up inside. I guess I must have had an overactive imagination. Well, either that or I had watched too many episodes of *I Love Lucy* because I was certain that if I got in it, I would get permanently trapped. I kept my distance from that machine.

By far, however, my favorite game to play in Grandma and Grandpa's private quarters was "Alligator." Uncle Dusty and Uncle Sandy would hide in the costume closets with the doors open and then turn off all the lights so it was pitch black. The rest of us would then start at the end of the hallway and run screaming down the corridor as my two uncles, "The Alligators," would let out a sudden growl and grab at our feet as we frantically darted by them. My heart would pound with excited fear. If we made it to our grandparents' bedroom without being caught, we'd fling ourselves on top of their big king-sized bed, which was the "safe" zone. If there were too many of us on the bed, what we called Grandpa's green leather "exercise slide" in the corner was also safe. But we had to have both feet up because if we touched the floor, we could still get tagged, not to mention of course, that the carpet was also "hot lava." The only thing we just had to be careful of, was that we didn't disturb any of Grandpa's cowboy boots, which lined every wall of their bedroom along the floor. I never remember tiring of this game. The fun was only over each time when Grandma or Grandpa would come down the hall and say, "Alright you kids, you're too noisy! Go ahead and play outside." Then the herd would disperse to go regroup somewhere else.

The ranch house seemed to ramble on forever, with so many different levels and places to explore. It was a kid's dream. The family room had a terrazzo tile floor that Grandpa had helped six of their kids embed their initials into with pebbles. Those tiles still remained there the last time I went through the house several years ago! That room also housed Grandpa's pool table that all the grandchildren knew NOT to mess with. Cue sticks were off-limits; however, it was fine to roll the balls around the table. I would nonchalantly sidle up to it, running my hand over the fuzzy green felt with the anticipation of collecting and releasing each ball into different pockets. Then I would scurry to the end, to see them drop into the tray one by one. I would do this again and again. In that same family room, Grandpa also kept a lot of his animal trophy heads on the wall. I know, I know. It is not acceptable today, but remember, this was the '60s, and it was all I knew. When I watched TV in this room, I would lie down on the lion rug and rest my head on top of his head. I would stroke his mane, separating it into smaller sections to braid. Grandpa had gone on an African safari and would bring back these kinds of things that I had now become very accustomed to. One of the most special keepsakes he brought back for me was a silver zebra pin, which to this day is very dear to my heart.

The room that Dodie and Debbie, my aunts shared, had a wall on the far side that was lined with stacks and stacks of comic books, each one piled a foot high. They also had a closet built into their wall, right next to the two or three stairs that descended into their bedroom. This closet was the perfect place to climb up into and hide. I would venture into that room a lot.

The backyard had horses, milk cows, cattle, pigs, chickens, guinea hens, pigeons, and peacocks. There was also a twenty-foot waterfall that Grandpa had built that tumbled over a small bluff. The house looked out over land as far as I could see, of undeveloped terrain with shrubs, boulders, and dirt roads, perfect for filming. I never tire of hearing Aunt Linda Lou telling me about the time she and her sisters took Nellybelle the Jeep, out for a forbidden spin when they were teenagers. Grandpa had warned his daughters not to take the Jeep out while he was gone. But they threw caution to the wind and did it anyway. As you can probably guess, they got the Jeep stuck over a big rock, and when they heard him return, no one wanted to go tell him. After many unsuccessful attempts to dislodge the Jeep, one of them finally ran and got Grandpa. He was not the least bit amused but got the Jeep out in a minute or so.

The next day, Grandma and Grandpa were out there filming, and the director stopped to study all the intertwined tire tracks over what was supposed to be a pristine dirt path for horses. So production stopped, having to wait for the crew to smooth out the tire tracks my aunts had made the day before. I think it's fairly safe to say, that the director was not amused either, and my aunts never tried that again.

At the ranch on warm days, we'd all end up in the pool, which was straight out the patio doors. Many games of Marco Polo were played in that pool, and it would become a flurry of splashing whenever Grandpa jumped in and played chicken with us. One time, we discovered a tarantula floating on top of the water. After we ran into the house screaming, Grandpa calmly stepped outside, grabbed the pool net, and fished it out of the water, throwing it over the fence. I was awestruck by his bravery and I felt safe when he was around.

Roy might have been a hero because he fought the bad guys in the black hats on-screen. He might have been a hero for standing up for the truth. He might have even been a hero for being a good example to children. But back on that warm summer day for me, he was most definitely my hero for getting that tarantula out of the pool.

Dad, grandma, and great-grandma Smith who raised Dad.

Nudie the Rodeo Tailor between two of his regular
customers, Gene and Roy.

Some of the family at Grandma and Grandpa's house.
Back row left to right: Aunt Mimi, Mimi's husband Dan, holding my newborn cousin Laurie, Aunt Linda Lou, my mom Barbara Fox holding me (also newborn), Grampa Roy, Grandma Dale, Dusty, Sandy. **Front row left to right:** Debbie, my sister Mindy, my sister Candie, Dodie.

This is Grandma and her younger brother, Hillman Jr. but everyone called him "Son." My Uncle Son was a whistle in a bag. Always grinning and good-natured, he smoked cigars and had a deep, gravely laugh. I adored him. He in turn, called me "Peanut" and would let me sit on his lap and "drive" his motorboat every summer on Lake Mead. Grandma Dale would get so exasperated with her "little" brother because Son teased her incessantly, and was as irreverent as they come. Uncle Son was married to Aunt Ben and they rode their matching motorcycles to our house now and then, which was always a treat. He was the regional manager of women's lingerie for Neiman Marcus, so we all got underwear or pajamas every Christmas. That was Uncle Son in a nutshell.

Left to right: Bennie (Son's wife) Roy, Dale, her brother Son.

Grandpa after his neck surgery with his three sisters from **left to right:** Kathleen, Cleda, and Mary. No DNA test needed here.

1955 Pasadena Tournament of Roses Parade, the year it rained. Roy and Dale had to be at the float barn by 4:00am to be hoisted up by a crane on to those floral horses in the photo. Of course, it was very chilly so the volunteers who were decorating the float kept bringing them hot coffee. After drinking more than a dozen cups, the parade was ready to begin but Roy desperately needed to find a restroom. There wasn't time, however, to unwire them without messing up all the flowers. He was panicked.

Fortunately, within minutes of rolling on to Colorado Boulevard, to wave at the crowds and the TV cameras, it began raining so hard, it became a real downpour and their costumes were completely drenched. Problem solved. Roy looked over at Dale and grinned. "Roy, you didn't!" Dale said. (True story as told to me by Grandma and Grandpa over coffee one morning.)

Chapter 7:

MAMA DALE AND DADDY ROY

Roy and Dale became grandparents for the first time in 1950, when my oldest sister, Mindy, was born, and shortly thereafter, my other sister, Candie. Well, "The King of the Cowboys" and "The Queen of the West," were still young and glamorous at 37 years old, and Dale wasn't too eager to be dubbed "Grandma" just yet. Since my sisters were almost the same age as the children Grandma and Grandpa were adopting, (who were actually our aunts and uncles), Grandma suggested to my parents that my sisters just call them, "Mama Dale and Daddy Roy." Easy enough. That seemed quite fine with everyone, that is, until eight years later when my dad's other siblings began having children, which was when I came on to the scene as well. By that time, the grandkid machine was officially up and running at full speed, so the terms, "Grandma and Grandpa," had become the accepted monikers of choice. However, my sisters were still calling them "Mama Dale" and "Daddy Roy" out of habit. Since I was the youngest of my parents' daughters, that's all I knew, so I just followed suit.

Then one weekend, my cousin Laurie and I, who were born just five weeks apart, were playing on the living room floor. Suddenly she turned to me and said curiously, "Why do you call them that?"

"What? Mama Dale and Daddy Roy?" I asked, feeling a little embarrassed. I had absolutely no idea what to say, so I just shrugged.

In the car on the way home from dinner, I asked my parents why we had to call them "Mama Dale and Daddy Roy" when all of my other cousins were calling them "Grandma and Grandpa."

"Is it a secret? Are they really our mom and dad? And if they are, then who are you?" I questioned apprehensively, knowing I was venturing into uncharted territory here.

Well, my parents never told me why, and even then, I remember thinking that something was fishy. Since I had no definite answer, and the terms, "Mama Dale and Daddy Roy" sounded so ridiculous to me, even at the wise old age of five, I decided that it was time to align again with my own kind, and go with "Grandma and Grandpa." Problem solved. After that, my sisters also went with the new name.

Years later, as an adult, I was going through a box in my garage, and I found an old birthday card to me, addressed from ... yup, "Mama Dale and Daddy Roy." It piqued my interest once again, so I decided to give that very same question another shot with my mom.

"This will be interesting," I mused.

My mom very matter-of-factly told me that Grandma had come up with those names herself because she felt that she was too young to be called grandma. There. She said it.

"Well, why didn't you just tell me that thirty years ago when I asked?" I laughed.

"I don't know," she shrugged.

With this cold case finally closed, I determined that all families are weird. Even the most wonderful ones have a little pinch of dysfunction. You just don't realize it until you're an adult. However, as trivial as this seems, I must say, that after the mystery of "Mama Dale and Daddy Roy" was solved, I've been sleeping much better now, thank you.

This is the age my grandparents were when I was born.

Grandpa signed my "autograph dog" *Daddy Roy*.

We all saw Grandma and Grandpa off on their cruise to Acapulco. The funny thing was, the ship's ballast tanks weren't working properly, so they cruised on down to Mexico at a 30-degree list. They ended up having to fly home. I am the littlest one in front.

The younger cousins at the Chatsworth Ranch. **Front row left to right**: Debbie, Sherry, Brian, Laurie, Kimmie, Dodie, Lisa. **Back row**: Me and Danny.

During these early family years, Grandpa would golf and go the shooting range with Clark Gable. Having many of the same interests, they became good friends.

Carl Switzer, who played Alfalfa in the original Little Rascals, always seemed to be in a pickle but he was like another son and Grandpa took him hunting a lot. You might recognize him from watching *White Christmas*. "Sure was a good lookin' kid."

Chapter 8:

TRIGGER AND BUTTERMILK

There is one question I get asked over and over, and I'm quite sure all of my cousins would say the same. *Was Trigger really stuffed?* As far as the stuffing goes, no. Trigger wasn't "stuffed," in the sense of the early 1700s, when it was the practice to fill the animal's skin with sawdust and sew it up like a bean bag. Ughhh. However, yes, Trigger was preserved. Grandpa had Trigger's measurements taken and an exact fiberglass mold, made of him while his horse was still alive. Then, when Trigger died in 1965, somewhere in his early 30s, the taxidermist stretched the skin over the mount and preserved him just like the animals you see in a natural history museum. "Mounted" is the correct term. Grandpa would get very particular about the terminology whenever anyone asked that question, so I thought it appropriate to answer here the way he would have.

I remember him also saying that Gene Autry thought he was crazy for spending that kind of money. But you see, that right there was the difference between the two friends. Gene was a successful and very shrewd businessman, whereas Grandpa was more sentimental. He couldn't bear to put his beloved horse in the ground, and he just felt that his fans would want to get a peek at Trigger as well if he was on display at the museum. Sure enough, Grandpa was right. Time after time, people traveling across the country on summer road trips, would come to the front door of the museum, right at closing time, and beg to just run in quickly, to see Trigger in his famous rearing pose.

I guess Trigger was kind of a big deal. He appeared in 88 movies and 100 episodes of their TV show. Back in his day, he was known as "The Smartest Horse in the Movies" and got top billing over Grandma, much to her chagrin. It really burned her bunny, so much so that she wrote a funny song about being billed last in the movie credits, even after a horse. At one point, Trigger even had his own comic book series, and fan club, getting 1,000 fan letters per week. He and Grandpa were also popular in Britain, Europe, Japan, and South America — where Trigger was known as "Tigre." Grandpa would laugh when he would watch himself and old Gabby Hayes speaking in foreign languages in the dubbed versions of his films.

Trigger had come from a small ranch in the San Diego area, which was partly owned by Bing Crosby. He was originally named "Golden Cloud," after the manager of that ranch, Roy Cloud. But when he was around three years old, he was sold to Hudkins Stables in the San Fernando Valley, which rented horses to the movie industry. Before Grandpa took a look at him, Golden Cloud had been ridden by Olivia de Havilland, who was Maid Marian in the 1938 movie, *The Adventures of Robin Hood*. When Grandpa got on him the first time, he knew that was the horse for him, and didn't even consider any of the others. Later, while on the set of his first movie, Smiley Burnette actually came up with the name "Trigger" when he commented, "Roy, as quick as that horse of yours is, you ought to call him Trigger." Grandpa, himself, would always quip, "He could stop on a dime, and give you nine cents change." So he ended up changing Golden Cloud's name to Trigger and buying him from the stables for $2,500, which was a lot of money back in 1938. Since he only made $75.00 a week at Republic, he had to make payments on Trigger, like putting a couch on layaway, I guess. "Best $2,500 I ever spent!" he would say.

Trigger, or "The Old Man," as he was fondly called by all who worked with him, was truly an amazing horse. Grandpa had a unique bond with him. They made many of his movies and his TV show together. However, when they went on tour, he didn't want to put Trigger through the exhaustion that naturally comes with long, rigorous travel, so he and trainer Glenn Randall trained another Trigger double to go on the tours. His name was "Little Trigger." While The Old Man was really smart and knew dozens of tricks, Little Trigger was the one who knew most of the tricks, but he was also very feisty. He was smart enough to know that he could get away with going rogue in the middle of a performance and that Grandpa would not reprimand him for it in front of an audience. One time, in the middle of a show, he bit Grandpa on the shoulder so hard, he tore his shirt a little and broke the skin underneath. Grandpa was so mad at Little Trigger that after the show, he stormed back to the paddock area to find him and give him the what for. However, Little Trigger saw him coming, so the horse started backing up as far as he could go until he hit the wall. Realizing he was now trapped, Little Trigger started doing every trick he knew; bowing, praying, counting, you name it. Grandpa stopped, shook his head, and had to laugh. Smart horse.

There was also a third double in the wings named Trigger Jr. who could do all the "dancing" as well as a few more palominos at the stables in case of emergencies. But the original horse forever remained Grandpa's "Trigger." There were little differences between all three Triggers, but The Old Man, I know, only had one left rear white sock and a wider blaze than the other two. Grandpa didn't like to admit to all of his young fans that there were actually three or more Triggers, because obviously, it might be confusing, upsetting, or even worse, ruin the magic for his young fans. But the reality was, in order not to run his horse into the ground over time, he needed to take some pressure off the original Trigger, who was his companion, and that's the Trigger I knew.

Buttermilk was originally named, "Soda." But one evening near the end of a long day of filming on location in Lone Pine, one of the wranglers, Buddy Sherwood, looked up and remarked,

"Look at those clouds, Dale! They look like clabber."

"You mean, buttermilk?" she said.

"Yeah! You should name your horse Buttermilk," he added.

She liked that. So he became "Buttermilk Sky," Buttermilk for short. He was rescued as a young colt, on his way to the slaughterhouse by a cattle farmer. He had been severely abused, which accounted for his somewhat nasty behavior. Apparently, they worked with him, which helped a little. They chose him as her horse in their television series, because his buckskin coat was a good contrast for Trigger's palomino color, especially when filming in black and white. Grandma admitted to me several times, that she was not an avid fan of Buttermilk. He was ornery and his gait was so rough, she said, that the caps on her fillings came out during a chase scene one time. She scowled and leaned in close. "That ole' horse was the reason for my hysterectomy! You know what I mean?" she laughed. Whenever the subject of taxidermy came up, she would also give Grandpa the side-eye, warning him that, if she died first, he had better not do the same to her, and put her up on top of Buttermilk.

Buttermilk may have been rough, but Grandma wasn't exactly a seasoned rider either, when she sort of fibbed her way into her first Western, "The Cowboy and the Senorita," with Grandpa. When asked if she knew how to ride a horse, she responded, "Well I am from Texas, aren't I?" But the minute Grandpa saw her, it was quite apparent to him that she didn't know one end of a horse from the other. She didn't even know which side to get on. But he held his tongue like a gentleman and didn't give her a hard time right away. He knew that Dale's big dream was not exactly to be in a cowboy movie, but she did "cowgirl up," and never complained. Later on, however, he would laugh and retell his first impressions of her by joking, "I never saw so much sky between a woman and a horse in all my life!" He suggested she take riding lessons, and he also ended up showing her some riding tips on set as they worked, so needless to say, she was a fairly decent rider by the time their show ended.

Buttermilk, being a quarter horse, was also faster out of the gate than Trigger. So whenever the director would call, "Roll cameras" on a chase scene, she would have to hold Buttermilk back, to let Trigger burst ahead as the star. There was never a doubt, however, about which one was the better horse. Trigger was a palomino stallion from a quarter horse cold-blooded mare and his sire was part thoroughbred, and though he was not as fast out of the gate, he could easily catch and outrun that old quarter horse Buttermilk every time when not shooting a scene.

Trigger was gentle enough that Grandpa could line his own children up on his back, from mane to tail, with confidence. He put us grandkids up on him as well. My earliest memory of being on Trigger was when I was almost four. One day at the Chatsworth Ranch, my dad and Grandpa asked if I wanted to take a walk to see Trigger down at the stable. Of course, I did!

By this time, Trigger was retired and enjoying a well-deserved life of leisure. Grandpa threw a saddle on him and led him out of the barn, asking, "Would you like to get on Trigger?" I don't remember saying yes, but I do remember wanting to get on, and before I knew it, Grandpa had picked me up and was gently hoisting me up on Trigger's back. Then they both stepped back, and grinned at me, as I sat there, holding onto the saddle horn with one hand, and touching his coarse, white, mane with the other. Though I was higher up in the air than I had ever been before, I felt oddly safe. Trigger just stood there calmly. My dad took some pictures, and I specifically remember looking back at them very curiously and thinking, *Well, I've got my horse. Where are yours?*

I knew he was Trigger, and that he had made movies. But little did I realize, I was sitting on a horse that was arguably the most famous in the country at that time. As an adult, I am now acutely aware that this was one of many adventures that I was privileged to have. In fact, now every time I step into a barn and smell fresh hay and horses, I am immediately transported back to a simpler time, where life was good, nothing was complicated, and my world, as I knew it, was safe. That always lets me know, that my happy upbringing has found a secure place in my heart, and a part of me will always remain that child.

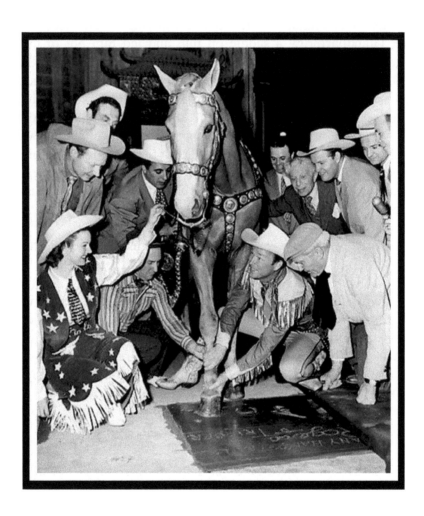

Roy and Trigger shared the spotlight at Grauman's Chinese Theater in Hollywood when they both put their hoof/foot prints in the concrete on April 21, 1949.

Over fifty years later, in the same spot at Grauman's on Hollywood Blvd, I am showing my sons their great-grandfather's handprints and Trigger's hoof prints.

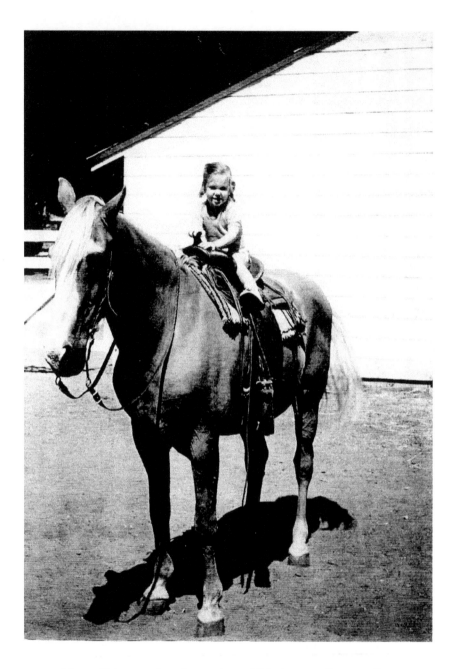

Me on Trigger when I was three. This is one of my earliest
memories.

"The Old Man" Trigger. He loved that horse.

Dale on Buttermilk.

Chapter 9:

IT WAS ALL FUN AND GAMES

Grandma and Grandpa were not filming their television show by the time I was born in 1958. We watched the reruns. But they still had a very busy schedule with personal appearances, TV guest spots, interviews, rodeos, state fairs, and what seemed like a million other things. With them, it wasn't a matter of having the time to spend with their family; it was a matter of making the time, which they did constantly. I always knew I mattered to them. I was worth going out of their way for, which gave me a grounded sense of family.

They would juggle their schedules when they could, to attend my school programs, graduations, birthday parties, family outings, and other activities I was involved in. We had a family tradition of putting on a little homemade Christmas pageant for all of our neighbors on our street every December, and one year, when we had a shortage of wise men, Grandpa filled in at the last minute as one of the three kings on the living room "stage" with all the kids. He stood there looking very serious and regal in his paper crown. I loved that about them. They could fly to Washington D.C. and spend the night at the White House one weekend, and then be sitting on my living room floor the next weekend, playing Old Maid with me.

Grandma and her mom, my Great-Grandma Smith, told me years later, that they would get so tickled when we played Old Maid together on the floor. I was about five or six, and I am sorry to say, that they loved playing with me because I cheated like a spinach weasel. My stealth plan was to bend the edges of the Old Maid card so much, that I would be able to see that card in their hand and avoid choosing it. Of course, at five, I did not have the foresight to realize that if I could see it, so could everyone else. But that's neither here nor there at this point. Furthermore, if I got dealt this dismal card, to begin with, I would push her up higher than the other cards in my hand, as if to say, "Pick me! Pick me!" and I was certain that they would. I was bold, daring, and just a little bit cocky.

Now I know what you're thinking. I should have felt some speck of remorse. But I didn't. That was the fun of it. Of course, my grandmother and great-grandmother would act as if they had no intention of picking the Old Maid card from my hand. But then, at the last minute, they would oblige, only to see me completely fall apart, giggling and rolling back on the floor. Trying to keep straight faces, they would admonish, "Now, Julie, you're not playing fair." Need I tell you that I never lost at Old Maid with them? Shocking. Interestingly enough, though, I never played this way with anyone else. It was just our special game, where the three of us spent most of the time laughing. I never tired of "our unspoken rules," and apparently, they didn't either.

We also had a bit of Roy Rogers merchandise around our house, because Grandma and Grandpa would get items to sample, and they would sometimes pass them along to us. At the peak of Grandpa's career, he had over 400 items on the market with his name or likeness on them. In fact, the only celebrity that had more merchandise was Walt Disney. There were Roy Rogers gun belts, shirts, ties, scarves, socks, boots, chaps, jackets, pants, hats, jewelry, pins, blankets, toothbrushes, cereal boxes, flashlights, action figures, bedspreads, rugs, slippers, robes, pajamas, wristwatches, towels, dishes, tea sets, lamps, coloring books, crayon sets, paper dolls, lunch boxes, board games, Colorforms, pens, puzzles, horseshoes, marbles, ranch play-sets, badges, purses, records, guitars, wallets, gloves, clocks, knives, cameras, dolls, cap guns, wood-burning sets, binoculars, comic books, harmonicas, footballs, Halloween masks, yo-yo's, mugs, pencil cases, backpacks, tents, lanterns, trading cards, toy chests, toddler underwear, dog food, feed bags, Kodak film, stoves, and even car parts ... to name a few.

I had a box of twelve Roy Rogers little yellow Golden Records, but instead of listening to a variety of their songs, and playing all of them, I decided that I liked Grandpa singing "The Swedish Rhapsody" the best, so I just played that one song over and over and over. I'm sure it was a little irritating for the rest of my family. Very early each morning, I would mount up on my Trigger rocking horse, waking the rest of the house up with the back-and-forth squeak of the springs and give Swedish Rhapsody a few spins. Maybe that's why my sister never wanted to share a room with me. I also had Roy Rogers and Dale Evans books, and other various toys. The Roy and Dale paper dolls were sort of fun, but I also thought they were a little bit creepy. I mean, who wants to see their grandparents in their underwear? I could never get their clothes back on fast enough.

My favorite of all, however, was my Roy Rogers Clubhouse. I would set it up in my room, or outside on the front porch in the summertime. It had metal rods that fit together to make the frame, and a log cabin printed canvas that fit over that frame. The windows were made of green netting with roll-down canvas curtains tied above. The door was a flap you could tie back, with the words "Roy Rogers Clubhouse" printed above. I had it down. I could set it up all by myself, and drag my little wooden table and chairs inside to prepare for my guests. My recipe was simple. Add a couple of dolls, maybe my friend Peggy from next door, some milk, cookies, and you've got yourself a party. When my grandparents came to our house, Grandpa would sometimes duck his head in. Sitting down in one of my tiny chairs, with his knees up to his chin, he would then order, and I would serve him "tea." It never occurred to me that I was entertaining the King of the Cowboys in a tent with his name on it. For me, I was having a tea party with Grandpa, in my Roy Rogers Clubhouse. I set up and took down that clubhouse so many times, that eventually, the canvas began to tear. It was probably tossed into a box with outgrown pedal pushers, and adjustable metal skates, bound for a thrift store. I'm not sure if there were more of these clubhouses made, or if it was just a tester that was never manufactured to sell, but, I have never seen another one like it since.

The older I get, the more I cherish these moments I had with the older generations of our family. I had my great-grandma Smith in my life until I was a senior in high school. I had my Grandpa Roy until I was forty years old, and my Grandma Dale until I was forty-three. So I guess that should answer another one of those questions I often get asked, which is, "Did you know them?" When that comes up, it makes me smile to say, "Yeah, a little bit." While I thought we were just having silly fun back then, we were busy making a lifetime of memories.

In 1956, President Eisenhower and his wife held a Roy Rogers themed birthday party at the White House for their grandson, David, who was turning eight. Not only was Roy Rogers the theme of the party, but he and his wife Dale Evans also attended as the special guests. Roy and Dale stayed overnight at the White House in the Lincoln bedroom. I have both the invitation the President sent to my grandparents, as well as the thank you note from President Eisenhower, expressing his appreciation that they both took the time out of their "busy schedules to visit the White House."

Roy and Dale at a fundraising event for the San Fernando Valley
Presbyterian Hospital in 1958.

Just a few of the hundreds of items Roy Rogers had on the market.

Chapter 10:

GRANDMA ON A LILY PAD

Grandma Dale was not exactly shy. Knowing her all of my life, I can tell you for a fact that it never crossed her mind to even try to fly under the radar when she walked into a room. She was the living definition of "outgoing." You never had to wonder what she thought or felt, because she would tell you — amusingly, whether you wanted to hear it or not. And though clearly not on purpose, she just seemed to cause a stir wherever she went. Her natural speaking voice was usually a bit animated and somewhat loud, so the whole room was often in on our private conversations. Her sense of style, especially when she was younger, was quite vibrant. She would often come to stay at our house, and I would stare with wonderment at her charm bracelet and other accessories that jingled, as well as all of her suitcases and bags that my dad would wrangle for her through our front door. I loved how glamorous she appeared, with a figure just like the Barbie doll she gave me.

Well, one Saturday, I woke up and was told by my dad that Grandma was performing at Marineland that day and we were going to go watch her. Now, unfortunately, Marineland of the Pacific is no longer there today, but from 1954 until 1987, it was a beautiful Southern California Oceanarium and tourist attraction located on 65 acres of the Palos Verdes Peninsula coast. Around the park were hotels, shops, and restaurants, which made it a trendy place to be during the '60s. The park was prominently featured in over a dozen television shows and movies, including two episodes of *The Chevy Show*, which my grandparents hosted, featuring an "Aquarodeo," in 1960. This particular day, however, was a few years later when I was almost seven, and Grandma was just making a solo appearance.

By the time we arrived, the outdoor stadium seating was full and there was standing room only to view the show, which was to happen there in the main lagoon. I stood with my parents by the fence off to the side and watched her perform. I thought it looked like fun. She was singing, and wearing a pink bathing suit, sitting on a giant lily pad in the middle of the lagoon, with mermaids doing synchronized swimming all around her. After her show was over, the park officials let us into the stage area to see her and chat, before enjoying the rest of the park for the day. It was sunny and breezy, and while I enjoyed watching Grandma, I was even more excited about getting popcorn and a miniature-sized plush dolphin to take home. I guess no matter what decade you live in, this fact remains the same; you can take your kids to see amazing, historical, or one-of-a-kind sights, but what they will remember most about the trip, is buying some little toy, or swimming in the hotel pool.

I guess I didn't really have the kind of grandma that stayed at home baking cookies. But the trade-off was, that I was quite possibly, the only one in my class who could say, "This weekend, I saw my grandma perform in her bathing suit on a lily pad."

Watching Grandma perform out on the lily pad at Marineland.

Grandma backstage after the show.

Grandma and Grandpa having fun with a sea lion.

Marineland was often used as a location for filming during the 1960s and 70s. Besides my grandparents using it for their show, the following list of television shows took advantage of this oceanside venue.

The Partridge Family
The Munsters
The Beverly Hillbillies
Emergency!
The Lucy Show

Batman
Sea Hunt
Six-Million Dollar Man
Wonder Woman
Live a Little Love a Little
(Elvis movie)

Chapter 11:

THE MAN IN RED

After Grandpa's work schedule slowed down, he found more time to play and have fun. He wasn't the type to sit around and play Scrabble or read a book. He immersed himself in just about every outdoor hobby he could find; racing boats, trap and skeet shooting, snowmobiling, race horses, hunting, fishing, and fast cars. One of the most fascinating of all of his friends was a portly gentleman with wavy, white hair, and lots of gold rings on his fingers. He was smooth and confident, and the conversation never lagged when he was around. He owned the used luxury car dealership in Encino that sold Jaguars and Aston Martins, and Grandpa was in business with him for a while, so I would see him at their ranch in Chatsworth. This man had a real name: Frank Millard. But he was better known to the people in the valley as "The Man in Red," because his advertising gimmick was wearing all red, everywhere he went; red shirt, red vest, red jacket, red cufflinks, red pants, red socks, red shoes, red hat ... He even dyed his dog's hair red, and of course, he drove a red car. I was wide-eyed and captivated every time he was around. I would stop what I was doing, and whisper, "There he is. The Man in Red!" I just knew he had to be the definition of cool.

Because of Grandpa's connection to this man and the automobile business, he had access to all kinds of cars he would drive around to test for fun. Once he even took us for a ride in an amphibious car, the same model that had been launched at the 1961 New York Auto Show, and sold from 1961 to 1968. We rode along the beach and then drove straight into the water. It tootled around like a boat — not a very fast boat — but nonetheless, we did cause quite a stir on the beach that day.

Another car he owned was a 1964 Pontiac Bonneville that Nudie Cohn, the Rodeo Tailor, had customized for him. Nudie also sold one to Elvis, which is now in the Country Music Hall of Fame Museum, back in Nashville, TN. There were 18 of these "Nudie mobiles" built between 1950 and 1975. Nine of them are known to survive today. In fact, Grandpa's showed up in an old rerun of the '80s TV show, *Hart to Hart*, last year. In the episode, the nefarious scoundrel drove up in it, to the Hart's home for a western-themed party. I recognized it right away and had to rewind it several times, just to enjoy the moment again. I also saw one of the other "Nudie mobiles" in an episode of *Jay Leno's Garage* on TV, where he showcases unique rides and the stories behind them.

These cars were intended to market Nudie's clothing business and attract attention. Well, they did, and the ones that are out there today still turn heads. The door handles were revolvers, the seatbelts were tooled leather cowboy belts, the inside upholstery was covered with silver dollars, and the center console was a leather, silver saddle. A pair of 6-foot steer's horns were mounted onto the front of the car, and when he honked the horn, it went, "Ahhooooga!" I only rode in that convertible one time in the back seat, when Grandpa took us for a little spin around the block before it ended up in the museum. Years later, at the Christie's auction, that car sold for over $250,000. Recently, I saw that Kid Rock just bought it, to add to his unique car collection. It was also featured on his album, *Born Free*. The album cover has a picture of Kid Rock sitting in what was Grandpa's car, in the back seat exactly where I sat 60 years ago. Weird.

Grandpa was always just a fun-loving, big kid who loved doing any kind of active sport. When Grandpa got older, the physical beating his back and neck took from doing a lot of his own stunts early on, and participating in all of those active hobbies, sort of caught up with him. Gene Autry would call the house, and he and Grandpa would be on the phone, both reclining in their La-Z-Boy chairs, and commiserating as old pals. I remember hearing Grandpa say, "My horse gets taller and my bowling ball gets heavier every year!" Grandma would shake her head and ask, "Well, Papa, was it all worth it?"

"Yep."

Grandpa out fishing with "The Man in Red."

Frank Millard and Grandpa were in business together selling luxury cars. Frank, more commonly known as "The Man in Red" is on the far right with the hat on.

I rode in the back seat of this "Nudie Car" once, with Grandpa driving.

Kid Rock in the one-of-a-kind Nudie Pontiac Bonneville he now owns. Back in the day, Nudie made 18 "Nudie Mobiles." Today there are believed to be nine still in use.

This was the model of amphibious car Roy had.

Grandpa was also an avid powerboat racer. He became vice president and co-owner of Yellow Jacket Boats in the 1950s.

Chapter 12:

THE STUMP TABLE

My grandparents had a lot of animals at the ranch in Chatsworth. Besides the barn animals, they had five dogs. Bullet, Bambi, Bowser, Bobo, and Mark. I guess they ran out of "B" names for that fifth dog. Bullet was obviously the German Shepherd, Bambi was a Chihuahua, and Bowser, well he was pretty gassy and always stunk like hogan's goat. Bobo was a big, gray poodle that Grandma always seemed a little annoyed with. But the dog that was by far my favorite was Mark, a German Shorthaired Pointer that Grandpa would take hunting. I would walk in the door and immediately look for him. Zeroing in on his location, I wanted him like a sack o' yams. Then I'd spend the next hour following him, and grabbing for his stumpy tail that was always wiggling, and just out of reach. He was so friendly that he didn't seem to mind this annoying little person tagging along behind him everywhere he went.

Well, in the living room, there was this small round table. The base was a block of white cement with little squares of turquoise-colored tile embedded in it. A tree stump was then mounted in the cement, and on top of that was a wagon wheel, finished off with a thick, round piece of glass for the table surface. I don't know where it came from, but it looked like someone had made it for them. I used to linger around that table when the dogs came in, and wait for it to happen ... and it always did. The first dog would come in and make sure the coast was clear. Then he'd make a beeline for this table, sniff the tree stump, and lift his leg. The next dog would enter, sniff, and do the same, followed, of course, by the parade of dogs, who quite obviously felt that this stump was the indisputable highlight of the living room, placed there entirely for their pleasure. Usually, by the time Grandma saw what was happening from the kitchen, it would be Bobo's turn at the stump, and he'd get busted. She would immediately drop whatever she was doing, grab a rolled-up newspaper, or anything she could find, and come charging out of the kitchen into the living room, wildly waving her arms. She'd holler at Bobo, while the other dogs scattered, every dog for himself. It was followed by an emphatic, "OUT! OUT!" after which she would mutter and return to the kitchen. She was so funny when she was upset, but I didn't dare laugh. It was sort of like a train wreck scene from a movie, that you just couldn't help watching over and over again, never tiring of it. I loved how she always vowed she would get rid of that table, but secretly I hoped she wouldn't ... and she never did while they lived there. However, when they moved from Chatsworth, I never saw the tree stump table again.

Many years later, I was watching the 71st Academy Awards, and Val Kilmer walked out onstage with a palomino, telling the audience that he had grown up on Roy Rogers' Ranch in Chatsworth. *Wait. I'm confused. Why don't I remember you?* I thought to myself. I did a double-take and called my Uncle Dusty. He verified to me that yes, indeed, the Kilmer family had bought the ranch from Grandma and Grandpa when they moved from Chatsworth to Apple Valley, CA in 1965. Once again, I marvel at the things I learn about my family long after the fact, or even, at times, from outside sources. Next time I run into Val I'll have to ask him if the stump table stayed with the house. Maybe at this very moment, it is still around somewhere living its best life.

I guess some people call my grandparents "legends." But this, my friends, is what real legends are made of — five male dogs, one tree stump, and a rolled-up newspaper. It just doesn't get better than that.

Roy teaching Dusty and Bullet how to shoot pool.

Mark didn't seem to mind that I tagged along behind him
everywhere he went.

Photo above: We used to go up to my grandparents' cabin at Big Bear Lake, CA. They actually filmed some of their movies and TV shows up there, so they became an integral part of the community. Grandpa and a friend owned Gray's Landing during the 1940s and '50s. Grandpa Roy told me that he would often go down to their little cafe on weekends and flip burgers to serve tourists. His buddy, Mel Blanc (voice of Bugs Bunny for Warner Bros) and his family would join them. **Below:** Grandpa on the dock, getting ready to take one of his boats out.

Chapter 13:

LITTLE ROBIN

In 1964, Grandma bought a mobile home at the beach, in Paradise Cove, Malibu, a beautiful beach town in Southern California, which has now become synonymous with multi-million-dollar Hollywood celebrity homes. However, back in the '60s, it was just a nice, rural beach to get away to, where she would go spend the weekend when she needed some alone time. The beach was her "happy place" and it invigorated her. Sometimes we would go out and visit, walking on the pier, watching people fish, having cookouts, or roasting marshmallows on the beach. We sometimes took turns swinging across the gully on the rope that hung from the Eucalyptus tree behind her mobile home.

Years later, my actor friend, Marty Kove, invited me to go have lunch with him in Malibu, and as we turned down this steep little hill to get to the beach, it suddenly felt familiar. I caught my breath as I realized where I was. "This was Paradise Cove! I hadn't been here since I was a little girl." The mobile home park is still there, and looks exactly the way it did in the '60s, except the little bait shack is now the Paradise Cove Beach Café. I have since been back many times, to kick off my shoes at one of their outdoor tables in the sand, and have lunch. It is even more charming than it was 50 years ago, and in the lobby of this little nautical café, among wall-to-wall photos of celebrities, there is a picture of Grandma and

Grandpa. When I see that, it feels as if I have come full circle back to my childhood.

Back in the day, Grandma also used her mobile home there to write her books. She wrote 29 in all, and years later, she gave my sisters and me a complete set of all of the books she had written. She signed all of them to each of us inside the front covers. However, upon opening each book, I discovered that in mine, and only mine, she had accidentally signed all of my books upside down and backward. "Ohh, Dale!" she started in on herself. But I stopped her mid-sentence. "Grandma. They're perfect!" I laughed. "I wouldn't want them any other way." Her first book, *Angel Unaware*, speaks of the only biological child they had together.

During her pregnancy, Grandma had caught a mild case of the measles, and Robin was born with Down Syndrome, along with some critical heart issues. The doctors broke the news to them that she probably wouldn't live long, advising them to put her in an institution so they wouldn't become too emotionally attached. That was the accepted practice during the 1940s. Grandma and Grandpa had no intention of following that advice. Robin was their daughter, a precious gift from God, and they were going to take her home and love her. Sadly, Robin died two days short of her second birthday.

Because of their outspoken stand with their Down Syndrome child, along with the book, *Angel Unaware*, that Grandma wrote, which became instantly a best seller, they were pivotal in educating the entire country, thereby causing a shift in public and professional attitudes toward children with Down Syndrome. They also continued to raise positive awareness and compassion for all children with challenges. As they became more vocal about Robin, more and more folks began bringing those children out to see their shows. Grandpa made sure that each venue they performed at would leave the first few rows reserved for such families. Then at the end of every show, they would side-pass on Trigger and Buttermilk, along the railing, to shake hands, sign autographs, and greet every single one of those families.

Although Robin was born eight years before I was born, and her time here on earth was short, her presence completely changed the Rogers family. There was more grace, more compassion, and a stronger love, allowing them to have a positive effect on the way America viewed children with special needs. Grandma and Grandpa began giving their time to help raise money for charity organizations and children's foundations. The Happy Trails Children's Foundation still exists today.

Grandpa would take Trigger into children's hospitals and visit the sick. He would put rubber shoes on Trigger's hooves, and cue the horse to go to the bathroom outside before entering the building. Then he alone, or sometimes with Grandma, would make the rounds, spending time with the sick children. Grandma and Grandpa would tell me years later that no amount of fame or money could equal the feeling of seeing those children's faces light up. If the child was blind, he would walk Trigger up to the bedside to bend his head down so they could feel his mane and run their little hands along his face. Then Grandpa would sing to them. My friend, and western singer Belinda Gail, performs a touching song, written by Joyce Woodson, called "He Sang For Me" which is based on the true story of one of those children Grandpa actually sang to. I challenge you to listen to it without tearing up. It's beautiful. Grandpa never left those hospital visits without an ache in his heart. Both he and Grandma felt it was their way of using their public voice as a way to help others. Then when my Uncle Sandy died suddenly in the Army overseas, they channeled their grief to do a USO tour to Viet Nam, coming alongside to support and bring encouragement to our service members overseas.

I was blessed to have these kinds of living examples of God's love. There is an old parable by an unknown author that is called, "Cracked Pots," which reminds me of the principles I was taught growing up. A water bearer in India had two large pots that he carried on each end of a pole over his shoulders, down to the river every day. One of the pots had a crack in it, while the other pot was perfect and always delivered a full portion of water to the water bearer's master, while the cracked pot arrived only half full.

For several years, this went on, with the full pot feeling very proud of its accomplishments, and the cracked pot feeling ashamed of its own imperfections, causing it to only accomplish half of what it was made to do. Finally, the cracked pot apologized to the water bearer, for leaking all the way back to the house every day, causing the water bearer to do more work.

But the compassionate water bearer responded, "Didn't you notice all of the flowers on your side of the path, that are not on the other side as we walk home? That's because I've always known about your flaw and used it for good. You see, I planted flower seeds on your side of the path, and every day you've leaked water, you have been watering them on our way back to the house. For several years now, I've been able to pick beautiful flowers to put on my master's table. Without you being just the way you are, he would not be able to enjoy this beauty."

The moral is simple. We each have our flaws. We are all cracked pots. But if we are faithful, not allowing our imperfections to determine our destiny, God can use us for good, in other people's lives. That, in a nutshell ... was my upbringing. My grandparents certainly weren't perfect. They had both left a trail of broken marriages, and self-centered aspirations along the paths of their lives. But when they finally surrendered their imperfections, mistakes, and even their egos to living a life committed to God, they accepted His grace, and freely gave grace to others. They were authentic with irresistibly charismatic personalities.

It would be impossible to write a book about my grandparents without at least mentioning their faith in God. Even those who didn't agree with their beliefs respected them. For they loved people with the kind of love that built bridges instead of walls, definitely a trait that endeared them to the public, which I witnessed time and time again throughout my life.

Dale pregnant with Robin at the beach with my parents.

Robin Elizabeth is the only biological child they shared together.

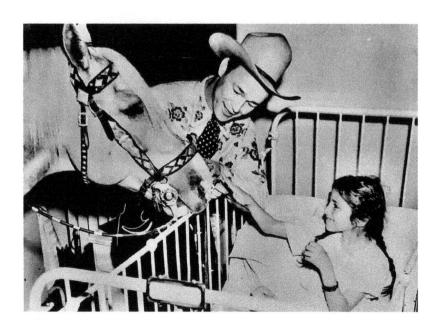

Above: Roy and Trigger surprising a little girl in the hospital. **Below:** 1966 USO tour to Viet Nam to encourage and entertain the troops. (Grandma is holding the doll she brought back for me.)

Chapter 14:

DEBBIE

The Chatsworth Ranch was a special place for me, and it was filled with people I loved and who loved me. It was my happy place. I never wanted it to end.

Then one summer it happened. It was August of 1964. My family was on vacation, pulling our travel trailer, "The Fox Den," as my dad called it. We were visiting all of the national parks throughout Arizona, Colorado, and Utah, and it was August 25th, my sixth birthday. My mom was going to ambitiously bake a cake in the trailer, and we would celebrate that night at our campsite, after arriving at the Grand Canyon. I was wiggling in my seat with excitement as we pulled up to the Ranger Station to check-in. But as we sat in the car, my mom noticed a chalkboard by the little guardhouse, and she whispered the message on it softly to herself, "Tom Fox, call your mom immediately." I didn't pay much attention to it until I saw the way my parents were exchanging concerned looks. My dad pulled over, and I watched as he got out of the car and walked over to the pay phone. I studied him intently from the station wagon. I could see by the look on his face, that his conversation was serious, and when he got back in the car, something wasn't right. My parents whispered back and forth, and then changed the subject, trying to lighten the mood, but they were preoccupied with something they weren't telling us. At the time, I couldn't have put words to the unspoken gloom, but I could certainly feel it, and it was unsettling.

When we got situated at our camp spot, we normally would have gotten busy setting up camp. I always loved that part of camping. My older sisters were usually asleep in the car by the time we got to our next camp spot, but I was always inquisitively wide awake. I didn't want to miss anything. My dad designated me, as his little helper every summer on our travels. Even at 6 years old, I got really good at guiding him as he backed the car hitch to the trailer, and I was proud of that.

But today, my dad didn't even ask me to help him. In fact, he didn't unhitch the rig at all. Instead, he set out a few chairs, while my mom hurriedly went inside the trailer to start on my birthday cake. We had an early dinner that night. My mom, in her rush, to finish the cake, iced it when the cake was still hot out of the oven, and all of the chocolate icing started to slide off, and pool around the bare yellow cake on the plate. My dad managed to snap a picture before the whole thing became a puddle, and we celebrated, but I was confused at all of the mixed messages. I opened a few presents, and then the hammer finally fell. "Girls, we need to pack up and get back home. Something has happened," my dad told us. "We'll talk in the car," my mom explained.

The weird mood plunged to a new level of ominous dread. "What?" I thought. "We just got here! What's happening?" We pulled out of the campground as night was falling, and there, sitting awkwardly between my parents in the front seat, the silence was deafening. My dad finally spoke. The horrible truth came pouring out, as he told us that my Aunt Debbie had just been killed in an accident. My brain was unable to accept this news. The church bus she had been on, coming back from the orphanage in Mexico, had blown a tire on the freeway near Carlsbad, CA, and had careened head-on into seven vehicles, including a station wagon coming in the opposite direction. All of the people in the station wagon were killed, along with Debbie, and her best friend, Joanne. They had been standing in the front of the bus, talking with their pastor, who was driving, and just before the tire blew, he had mentioned they had better go back and sit down.

I couldn't believe what I was hearing. My perfect little world was shattered. She was only six years older than me, and I adored her. Debbie was vibrant, outgoing, and full of life. I had to accept that Debbie was never coming back but that was too much for me. I laid my head on my mom's lap until her jeans and my cheek were wet with my tears.

We drove all night in silence, back to Chatsworth. When we walked in the kitchen door, Grandma was sitting at the big, round table sobbing with her head in her hands. Grandpa wasn't there, because he was still in the convalescent facility in Bel Air, recovering from neck surgery, and battling a staph infection. Grandma had called and adamantly stressed that the hospital staff was not, under any circumstances, to let him turn the TV on in his room, because of course she didn't want Grandpa hearing it on the news. The whole scene shook me to the core and has forever been imprinted in my memory. The ranch, my safe place, no longer felt safe, and it scared me to watch all of the adults in my world, fall apart. They weren't supposed to do that. I ran out of the kitchen, through the living room, and down the stairs to Debbie and Dodie's room. I crawled into their closet and hid among their clothes, feeling fearful and bewildered, I sobbed from somewhere deep inside. Life was never the same for me at the Chatsworth Ranch. That chapter was now closed. I guess you could say that the summer of my sixth birthday was a memorable one.

To this day, I still think of Debbie anytime I get on a bus. It may not make complete sense, but ever since then, I make it a point to avoid sitting in the first few rows of any bus. I have always impressed upon my own children and husband to do the same. That event remains one of my most unsettling experiences ever.

I watched my grandparents both gracefully deal with grief and disappointment over the years, more than any parents ought to have to face. And in the long run, my strong, determined Grandma, whom I had witnessed falling apart that awful day, taught me through her words, yet more importantly through the way she lived, that God is good, all the time. But sometimes life is just excruciatingly hard. You have to cry, even sob ... and that's ok.

Debbie and Dodie shortly before Debbie died.

We had just arrived at our camp spot at the Grand Canyon. It was my 6th birthday. I am posing with my new ball, but even through my smile, I sensed something was wrong. Shortly after this, we were back in the car, finding out that Debbie was gone and never coming back.

Grandma holding it together at Debbie's funeral without Grandpa who was still in the hospital. **Pictured with her:** Dodie, Dusty, and manager Art Rush standing behind.

Chapter 15:

WHERE ARE THE APPLES?

In 1965, after Aunt Debbie was killed and laid to rest at Forest Lawn Cemetery in Glendale, Grandpa was plagued with sadness over the many painful memories of her everywhere he looked at the Chatsworth Ranch. Before her death, he had bought a beautiful piece of property in Hidden Hills, which he had been fixing up for the family to move there. It was just over the hill from Malibu, and he had been taking Debbie and Dodie there with him on the weekends. So not only did the Chatsworth Ranch have difficult reminders, but now also this new ranch they were to move into was depressing for him as well. I developed an uneasiness being around Grandpa during this time. After his neck surgery, he had to wear a tall, stiff neck brace for quite a while. He looked ominous to me, and it continued to remind me of Debbie's death.

He had just moved Trigger out to this new ranch, but Trigger died too shortly thereafter on July 3, 1965. It had not even been a year since they had buried their 12-year-old daughter, and now his beloved horse was gone. He couldn't even bring himself to tell the family until a year later, but it was obvious that he was not himself. His doctor told him that maybe a move up to the high desert with its fresh air might be good for him and his family. So he sold both ranches and headed for Apple Valley, a town just outside Victorville, California.

At that same time, my dad was in danger of possibly losing his job. He taught band, orchestra, and choir at Rosemont Junior High School, but Glendale Unified School District was making cuts to the music program. If that didn't get our attention, the city of Los Angeles also decided to build the 210 freeway where our home stood. So we were told that our house in Montrose was in the way and would have to be removed. Removed? Just hang a noodle on my ear. What does THAT mean? My life had turned from a Saturday morning cartoon into a gothic novel. Besides, we lived right next to Descanso Gardens where we would go on Sunday afternoons to feed the ducks, and it was one of my favorite places. We can't move! Well, my dad got two job offers north of Los Angeles, one in Santa Barbara and the other in Los Gatos. He took the job in Los Gatos, and the moving truck arrived.

Meanwhile, my grandparents' hopes of starting a new chapter in the high desert town of Apple Valley were crushed three months later when Uncle Sandy died suddenly at 18 years old.

Sandy had gone into the U.S. Army and had been deployed to Frankfurt, Germany. He had just earned his stripes, and his buddies took him out to celebrate. Sandy, being a follower and wanting to fit in, drank too much, passed out, and was found unresponsive the next morning. I was seven, but I don't remember the events around his death as much as I did with Debbie; I think it was for a few reasons. I had been closer in age to Debbie. Sandy had been gone overseas for a while, and we weren't at the ranch every weekend anymore, because we had all scattered and moved away. But I did know once again that the familiar dark cloud had drifted over my family, and it was almost too much, and too soon for my grandparents to bear. It scared me that death had become a familiar topic in my family. Even though I might not have been in the middle of discussions, I overheard a lot and I felt anxious.

The first home they bought in Apple Valley was a one-story, rambling house that was on a frontage road right next to the highway. We called it the Highway House. The first time we drove down from our new home in Los Gatos for a visit, I was curious about this place called Apple Valley. As we got closer, I determined that I would be the first one to spot all the apple trees in this valley of green meadows I imagined. But the scenery was becoming more and more desolate. "Where are all the apple trees, Dad?" I questioned. There was nothing but high winds, sand, tumbleweeds, and cactus. Not even a blade of grass anywhere. We got off the highway and turned sharply onto a frontage road. About a half-mile down that road, we made a left turn into a circular driveway, which had a house with a vaulted, pointy roof, blanketed with little, white sparkly rocks on top that jutted out over the front door. I was crestfallen. "This is so strange," I whispered to myself, lots of dirt everywhere, with cars and trucks rushing by at high speeds. I missed Chatsworth.

Despite the obvious absence of apples, in this place called Apple Valley, it did become their new home and we all adjusted. We all still got together for holidays and special occasions at their house. The mail obviously found them because their huge Christmas card basket would still fill up with interesting greeting cards and photos of actors and their families, famous news people, the President himself, and other celebrities, which always made it fun to explore. Bob and Dolores Hope sent them a huge poster one year in a decorated Christmas tube. It was a calendar for the upcoming year with photos of them all over it. When Grandma said she didn't know where she was going to put it, she looked over at me and said, "Here Sugarfoot. Why don't you take it." So I stared at Bob and Dolores Hope on my bedroom wall for the whole next year.

I did have a certain fascination with two parts of the Highway House. The first was the doorknob on the front door. It was made of brass, round with ridges in it like a beach ball and it was the size of a cantaloupe. It looked like it had been lifted right out of Fred Flintstone's house in Bedrock. The first time I tried to open the door, I was confused.

"The doorknob doesn't turn, Baby," Grandma said. "Just push on it." I quickly discovered that she was right. It didn't turn. If the door was unlocked, I would just have to grab it with both hands and throw all of my weight against the door. The door would then sort of fly open after a couple of pushes, spilling me onto the living room carpet. If I was inside, I still had to pull pretty hard on the door handle to open it. I developed this kind of odd fascination with this weird doorknob. It became a procedural thing for me. Obviously, when we'd arrive, we had to wait for someone to answer the door. But then I would usually find some reason to go back out to the car, so I could come back in and open this stone age door all by myself, which of course became part of the mystique every time we visited. It's odd, the kinds of nostalgic things we remember. I would love to find that doorknob now and mount it on my wall or something, just for a nostalgic conversation piece.

The second thing I liked about that house was the bottle room. The entire outside wall was made of concrete and stucco with green bottles embedded in rows, and when the sun shone through them, the room was lit with an eerie green tint. In my imagination, it was my cave. I would hide notes inside the bottles and then come back an hour later to see if they were still there. I know, I was a weird little kid.

But the best part of their house was that shortly after they moved there, they brought my great-grandma Smith out from Texas to live with them. They had moved her from her home of sixty years in Italy, Texas, where we used to visit her. She, of course, missed her home but was thrilled to see my dad more, now that we were all in California. After all, she had raised him on their farm in Texas for several years of his life. He grew up calling her "Mom," and calling my grandma, "Frances," which is another whole story.

We made many memories during these years. Grandma Dale was always fun to be around. But she could also be horrifyingly embarrassing. She would take me shopping at the mall, and several times it happened at the register right in front of the sales clerk. She would whiff, puzz, puffoon, or pop an air biscuit, whatever you want to call it. Then she'd raise her hand up high, turn and address anyone who was standing nearby and declare loudly and matter-of-factly, "Sorry! That was me! That was me!"

"Grandmaaaw!" I'd groan in my whisper voice, as I'd turn and lunge toward the nearest clothing rack to look busy. Things like this absolutely did not faze her a bit. I do have to say, it was never a dull moment with her.

Then there was Grandpa. It seemed there wasn't anything he couldn't do when it came to any kind of physical sport. They still had their cabin by the lake up in Big Bear, where we could boat and fish. During the winter, he took us for rides on his snowmobile. He was a pretty good bowler for a cowboy. He joined a local bowling league, and even played in several seasons of a television series called, *Celebrity Bowling*. My favorite was when his partner was Don Adams (star of the old *Get Smart* TV show), which I would later get to know personally. They played against Bob Newhart and George Foreman.

One day, he took a good-sized batch of us grandchildren to the local bowling alley to teach us how to bowl. This created quite a stir, as other patrons peered over the bowling ball shelves, taking pictures of Grandpa helping each one of us when it was our turn. Orange soda, Pixy Stix, and gutter balls were plentiful that day, and for Grandpa, it was much like herding cats. We were everywhere. I can't recall how much we actually learned from our bowling lesson, but I do know we wore him out because he came home and took a nap.

Grandpa needed something to do here in this new place. Grandma said, "Roy, you have so much STUFF! We have no more room. You need to get yourself a museum or something to store all of your things!" So he did. He bought the old bowling alley in Apple Valley just down the highway from the house, remodeled it, and the first Roy Rogers and Dale Evans Museum was born in 1967. It soon became Grandpa's "happy place" and he loved going over to the museum in the early mornings before it opened, to just stroll through it himself and reminisce. He delighted in showing us his newest additions and displays as his museum unfolded. The museum was special for all of us because many of the things we had grown up with from the Chatsworth Ranch ended up in the museum. It was sort of a three-dimensional family scrapbook that all of us could enjoy. Rugs, furniture, personal items, and to my delight, even Lazy Susan was there.

They lived in the Highway House for eleven years until I went to college in 1976. In all that time, I never saw any apples. Shortly after, they moved the museum to a more accessible location in nearby Victorville on Highway 15. It remained there for twenty-seven years until they passed, first Grandpa in 1998, and then Grandma in 2001. A few years later, our family had a decision to make. All of our parents voted, and we moved the museum to Branson, Missouri.

There were a lot of opinions, as to whether or not we should have moved the museum. I can only say this, after both Grandma and Grandpa died, the museum faced a steady decline in visitors, because people had been coming there, hoping to meet Roy, who was at the museum almost every morning. Even Patrick Swayze made the trip up to the museum and was like a little boy on Christmas morning when he got to meet Grandpa. He turned to my cousin, Shawna, and said in a squeal, scrunching up his face, "I just got to meet Roy Rogers!" With them both now gone, the museum was struggling.

I heard Grandpa say several times, "After we are gone, if the museum starts costing you money, then liquidate everything and move on." So the family thought, rather than closing it, it was worth giving the museum one last shot in a brand new location, which already drew busloads of tourists.

When we moved it to Branson, Missouri in 2003, it lasted for six more years before closing for good. It never really bounced back after the 2007 recession, and it was losing money. No one wanted to buy the museum collection in its entirety, so everything was auctioned off piece by piece at Christie's Auction House in New York City in 2010. Though it was heartbreaking to watch some of their personal items being bid on, and then scattered all over the country, the auction overall was positive. It was heartwarming to know that so many people all across America, and even other parts of the world, loved Grandma and Grandpa so much that it was important to them to have a little piece of their lives.

And for us family? After all, it is just "stuff." With the right perspective, it's much easier to let go. The way I see it, our memories can never be taken away or bought, and as far as the material things, none of us will be leaving this life, towing a U-Haul anyway.

Above: We moved to Los Gatos up in Northern California, where my grandparents would then come stay with us. That woman directly in back of me? Oh, that's my mother, apparently not wanting to blow her cover by taking one step to her left for the photo. **Below:** Grandma and Grandpa's first house in Apple Valley was right off the highway, so we called it "The Highway House."

Sitting with Grandma and three of the dogs in the living room. **Left to right:** Bowser, Bobo, and Bambi.

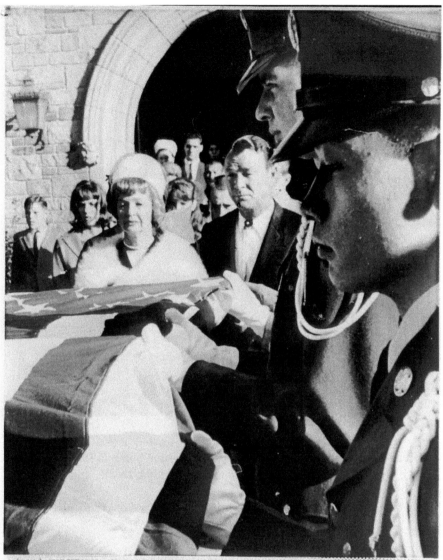

Uncle Sandy's funeral service at Forest Lawn in Glendale, CA

Great-Grandma Smith moved from her longtime home in Italy, Texas to live with them. **Left to right:** Grandma, Grandpa, Dodie, and Grandma Smith.

Grandpa joined a local bowling league. He also made several guest appearances on the Celebrity Bowling TV series, starring with Bob Newhart, George Foreman, Don Adams, and here with Flip Wilson.

Grandma used to tease Grandpa, saying that he had so much in storage, he ought to build a museum for it. So, he did. "Well Papa, you finally got your museum!"

The second location of the museum in Victorville.

Roy at the museum in Victorville with Patrick Swayze.

The last museum after moving it to Branson.

The day we all went to Catalina Island and grandma was so worried I would get sunburned. Why me, and no one else? Much to my annoyance she went to a souvenir store, bought a hat just like hers, and made me wear it. Of course, Grandma Mabel is lurking in the background, not wanting to even be in the photo. Quite a group.

Chapter 16:

BIRTHDAYS

The doorbell rang. When I opened the door, sitting on the front porch was a box as big as me. It read, "To Julie Fox, From Roy and Dale Rogers." My eyes widened as I dragged it inside. I had never seen a box this big, addressed to just me. It was 3 days before my 8th birthday, but this was truly peculiar. My grandparents were not the kind who spoiled us, so to say I was excited, was an understatement. Mom let me open it, knowing that three days of waiting, was a long enough time for me to drive her crazy. So we began the suspenseful excavation down into the treasures.

A small jewelry box, with a "Little Kiddles" locket inside, a kaleidoscope, a new jump rope, a dozen Disney records, a stack of children's books, a black and white kitty-kat clock whose eyes rolled back and forth, and a huge vinyl dollhouse, complete with princess furniture and a carrying handle on top. I was speechless. By noon that day, I had my thank you note written, addressed, and stamped, ready to go. You just never knew what to expect, and I loved that about Grandma and Grandpa. That kind of gift had never happened before and was never to happen again, which is why, to this day, my eighth birthday will always be remembered as the most unexpected.

Grandma always kept a calendar of everyone's birthdays. I don't ever remember her forgetting my birthday, even once. Early on, she tried her best to give actual gifts to us all. But that became more and more difficult the older we got. There were so many of us grandchildren, sixteen in all.

One Christmas, for all of us granddaughters, she called down to the nearest JC Penney store and ordered each of us sweaters, all in a size medium. But as time went on, even mass buying became unmanageable. Christmas consisted of a box of Harry and David pears and a yearly subscription to *Guideposts*. She would then send us a check inside a sweet little Christmas card, "With love from Grandma and Grandpa."

As the great-grandchildren arrived, she fine-tuned her organization even more by sending all of the birthday cards out on the first of each month. So if your birthday was on August first, your card was a tad bit late. But if your birthday was like mine, at the end of August, my card was always three weeks early. But again, she never missed a birthday.

Now as all of my cousins can attest to, Grandma was always on the run, and if she couldn't find just the right card, and didn't have time, she would just use another kind of card, adding things or crossing things out, to make it exactly how she wanted it to look. Her motto was, "Oh, I can fix this." More often than not, I would get a birthday card from her on Valentine's Day with a big heart, hand-drawn in pen around whatever was on the front of the card, and inside, the word, "Birthday" was crossed out and replaced with "Valentine's Day" written in her handwriting. These "Valentines" were sweet and hilarious at the same time. Oh, how I loved getting those!

When I went away to college, Grandma started sending me cassette tapes instead of handwritten letters. I loved it because she would just chat about everything on the tape. Even the smallest details of what she was doing at the moment in the kitchen would segue into a TV guest appearance that she needed to find a dress for. She talked to me on those tapes like a steady stream of consciousness. If she dropped something on the floor, while the tape was running, I'd hear her mutter, "Oh Dale!" Her letter tapes to me were so organic, and I would grin with anticipation when I'd find them in my mailbox. She was genuine. They both were. What you saw was what you got.

I remember one year, I'd forgotten about HER birthday, on October 31. I was in my dorm room studying when I suddenly heard the radio hosts chatting about Dale Evans and that it was her birthday today. They went on to discuss if she was still alive or not. I quickly closed my book, and muttered, "Oh yes! She's very much alive, and I must call her right now." I ran to the phone to call her. I have to admit, getting little reminders like that on the radio, was definitely a perk of having a celebrity for a grandparent.

Even with sixteen grandchildren, Grandma never forgot a birthday.

Always looking to try something new in marketing, Roy entered the restaurant business in the late '60s. The Marriott Corp. approached Roy about the use of his name. The first Roy Rogers fast food restaurant opened on April 6, 1968 in Falls Church, VA.

By the 1980s several hundred restaurants had been established nationwide, reaching 650 at its peak. Roy was paid for the use of his name and also for his personal appearances at the restaurants. As of 2023, though there are only 40 restaurants left in six states on the east coast, the restaurant chain still boasts 54 years of longevity, and is returning to the Cincinnati area with ten new locations. **Below:** Roy and Dale pictured under the carport at the ranch in Chatsworth. Funny to see them "cooking" because neither one of them were good cooks.

Chapter 17:

THE ROCK COLLECTION

When I was 9 years old, I was fascinated with rocks. Everywhere I went, I looked for another gem to add to my collection. You must know that I am using the word, "gem," very loosely and that my "collection," to the untrained eye anyway, was merely a box of common rocks. Nonetheless, to me, they were gems, and I was proud of my growing collection. In fact, I was so proud that one weekend, I brought my fine specimens over to the house to show Grandpa. *I'm going to show him my gems. This is just the sort of thing he will love!*

We turned off the highway onto the frontage road that led to their house. Grandpa was in his favorite rocking chair watching TV. He got up when we arrived, and after greetings and kisses, which I always hated from Grandpa because his smooches were always wet. I would wipe them off my mouth with the back of my hand as I walked away, being sure, that he didn't notice, so as not to hurt his feelings. When all of the family dispersed into different rooms, he sat back down in his rocking chair. I plopped down on the floor and scooted up beside him with my box.

We sat there in silence watching some show together and when the commercial came on, he looked down at me sitting there beside him, pointed to my box, and said, "Whatcha got there?"

"Gems," I said very matter-of-factly.

He turned off the TV. "Ohh? Let's take a look," he said.

I proceeded to show him every gem in my collection, one gray stone after another, explaining where, when, and why I had saved each one. God love him. He listened patiently to my painfully long presentation. Then his eyes squinted, and he shot me that mischievous grin that I loved so much, and said, "Bring your box and come with me." So off I pattered after him, out to the garage. We stood in front of his workbench, as he gently took the box from me, and placed it up on the long, sawdust-covered table strewn with pieces of wood, leather, bits of chain, and some bumpy round rocks he called "geodes."

"Watch this!" he said. He took an ugly round rock, which he had already cut open, and he spread the two halves apart, revealing the stunning crystals inside.

"But it was so bumpy and ugly on the outside!" I laughed.

"I know!" he said as he pulled another geode out. "They're made that way. Look at this one here!"

I was completely awestruck, as he began to show me the most beautiful rocks I had ever seen; geodes, agates, obsidian, quartz, all right there on his dusty old workbench! He even showed me a few that he had already polished and cut into shapes to make bolo ties with.

"Whoaaaa! You got good gems, Grandpa!" I exclaimed. I was so intently focused on each rock that I didn't notice he was putting all of them one by one into my box as we talked. Not until he put the lid back on my box, and I picked it up, did I notice that it was now very heavy. He had put all of HIS treasures into MY box.

He smiled, and said quietly, "Why don't you take these, and add them to your collection."

He was a man of few words, finding it hard to express his emotions. I put the box down and hugged him tight. "Thanks, Grandpa!"

It's been 50 years, and I still have the rocks he gave me so long ago. I take them out every once in a while, and the memory of that afternoon with Grandpa at his workbench comes flooding back like it was yesterday. I was rich, and I felt it. Not because I had been given beautiful stones, but because I knew my grandpa loved me. And that is priceless. Better than gems

.

Grandpa in his favorite chair in the living room, which was exactly where he was sitting when I sidled up next to him on the floor with my "gems."

The rock collection Grandpa gave me when I was nine still brings a smile to my face, remembering our serious conversation about "gems" that day in the garage.

Chapter 18:

THE JONATHAN WINTERS SHOW

It was Fall of 1968, I was ten and sitting at the kitchen table finishing up my homework. Suddenly, from the other room, I heard my older sister, Mindy, exclaim, "Hey! Look what it says in the TV Guide! Roy Rogers and Dale Evans and all of their family join Jonathan Winters on a CBS Christmas Special in December." I put down my pencil and added my two cents, "But how can that happen? No one even told us!" Well, sure enough, my dad called Grandma, and apparently, she just hadn't gotten around to letting the family know yet.

It was true. This was the second TV Christmas Special we were going to be on with Grandma and Grandpa. However, I didn't remember *The Dinah Shore Show*, because I was barely 3 years old when it was taped. I was ecstatic to have another go-around at it.

My mom got busy and sewed my sisters and me similar dresses in the same fabric, to wear on the show. This was also to be our first time flying on a plane. So many new things all at once. I was thrilled when I discovered I would be missing three days of school for this big adventure. But reality settled in when I found out we still had to attend school while there. What? Are you serious? Yes. All of us who were under 18 years old, were required by law to get a work permit, as well as attend school with a set teacher while we were at the studio. The day before we left, my fifth-grade teacher, Mrs. Callisch, handed me a packet of work, which I reluctantly took, and off I went.

The day we boarded our flight, we all dressed up like we were going to church. Our good friends, the Friesens, saw us off at the airport and took our picture after they hung festively wrapped candied leis around our necks. The flight attendants back in the sixties were still called "stewardesses," a title that carried an alluring mystic. I wistfully watched three of them as they breezed by the ticket counter, laughing and chatting nonchalantly, as they rolled their little travel bags behind them. They nodded politely to the employee behind the counter as they passed. I was awestruck by these glamorous, young women that looked like models in their pink and orange hot pants, with matching bubble hats, and high heels. During the flight, I sat by the window and ordered a Coke with ice. I played with my tray table, slid the shade up and down at least 27 times, and snapped off a whole roll of black and white pictures of clouds. There might have also been a little light kicking on the seat in front of me too, so, to whoever was sitting in front of me during that flight, I'm so sorry.

We, of course, had bigger things to think about than flying on a plane. During the flight, my dad leaned over to remind me that we had a song to sing and asked if I had memorized my music. I had, but I probably would have said yes even if I hadn't, because I've always been the kind of person who "wings things" at the last minute. Grandma and Grandpa had decided that my immediate family (Dad, Mom, me, and my two older sisters) would perform the song "Bless This House" on the variety show.

On our first day in Los Angeles, the five of us went over to CBS where the orchestra was taping their instrumental background for the song track. We listened to them rehearse it once. After that, the director asked us to sing our parts all the way through once with the orchestra. Then the third time, they recorded the whole song with my family of five being accompanied by this 30-piece orchestra. That's it. Rehearsal over. It was pretty amazing. Then when the show was taped on stage, we were told that we would be lip-syncing the song in front of the live audience, after which the whole Rogers family would then join in with us to sing "Let There Be Peace on Earth."

The next few days were busy with rehearsing, and all of us cousins attended school on set. It was really just an extra room down the hallway from the soundstage, that had about a dozen desks inside, and a studio teacher waiting for us. She made it clear that we were to sit quietly and do the schoolwork we had all brought. *Ohhhh,* we thought. *So this is like a study hall.* After a few minutes, of course, I had to use the restroom. After getting directions, I set out, taking the long way. I guess it's fairly obvious by now that I was an inquisitive child. I stopped at the wig salon, wardrobe, and several other soundstages where one was in the process of taping a show. I knew enough to know that the red light near a closed door, whether flashing or static, meant, "You better not!" I meandered between large painted sets on dollies. It was a cavernous maze that seemed to have no end or ceiling. However, I soon realized that I needed to stay close to the main aisle, which seemed to be the thoroughfare to find my way back. Eventually I did. The teacher gave me a stern glance when I walked back in the door, so I immediately dove into one of my books. All things considered, "set" school turned out to be not really that bad.

On the day of the taping, Grandma and Grandpa, the six kids, their spouses, and all thirteen of us grandchildren, met at what used to be called CBS Television City, there on Fairfax by the old Farmer's Market in Los Angeles. The guard gave us a pass to park, and we all went to our dressing rooms to drop off our clothes. We were told we could go to the soundstage and watch the other guests on the show rehearse, while we waited for our turn. Frank Gorshin, who played The Riddler on the TV series "Batman," was practicing his song, so we sat quietly in the first two rows of the audience seats to listen. Red Skelton heard Grandma and Grandpa were there with their whole family, so he popped in on his break, interrupting rehearsal to say hi. A young adult singing group called, "The Kids Next Door" then got up and blocked out their number as they rode large hoppity-hop balls all over the stage. Finally, it was time for The Rogers Family. The crew quickly changed the stage to a Christmas Living Room scene, and the assistant director proceeded to assign all of the grandchildren jobs. Some of us were playing with presents under the tree, others were over on the floor playing a board game. The funny thing was, Aunt Linda Lou and Uncle Gary happened to be babysitting a friend's child the week of the taping. So he had just come along with them and was counted in as one of the grandchildren to be on the show. My other cousins and I didn't even notice the extra kid at the time, and it wasn't until years later, looking at the family photo the studio took of us on set, that I asked, "Wait. Who is that?!" My cousin Sherry replied, "Oh, that was the little boy we were babysitting for a few days." I bet he's had quite a story to tell all these years.

Anyway, my sister, Candie, and I were told to look busy arranging the flowers and garlands on the fireplace. Then we were instructed that when Jonathan Winters entered, wearing his Viking hat, we were to stop and move over to the couch to sit all around him, so he could tell us a story. Then after that, the adults would slowly saunter onstage, there would be a bit of dialogue, and we would do the singing part the five of us had practiced, followed by the big family number. Lastly, there would be some closing dialogue, and Mr. Winters and Grandma and Grandpa would bid the viewers a Merry Christmas to end the show. The director said we would run the show through twice, for two different live audiences, and then it would be a wrap.

We all went to our dressing rooms to get ready. I zipped up my pretty blue dress with the matching belt and fabric button in front. The silver flecks in the dress sparkled in the mirror under the makeup lights. My mom let me wear a little bit of makeup and for the first time ever, I was allowed to wear white fishnet stockings. "Ok, I am almost a stewardess," I whispered to myself. When the dust settled from all the Clairol, I had enough hairspray on my hair to stop a bullet. It was a bit of mayhem backstage with all of us laughing, poking, jumping, and chattering, with adrenaline, while our parents straightened our clothes and tried to shush us.

The man with the headset on came back to tell us we were on next. Miraculously on cue, we entered the stage and took our places. I was staring out into a sea of organized confusion with TV cameras on wheels, black cables tangled everywhere, gaffers, grips, cue cards, sweltering hot stage lights, a boom operator sitting up high, and the live audience staring back at us. But when I turned the other direction, there I was, standing in a lovely, calm living room, with poinsettias at my feet, and a realistic fire in the fireplace, in the hearth, which was draped in Christmas garlands that sparkled with tiny white lights. Close by was the inviting couch with a cowhide rug peeking out from under it. Across the room was the beautifully decorated Christmas tree, taller than I had ever seen in my living room at home. It was dressed and ready with a rainbow of colored lights and ornaments, with tempting presents underneath. I knew they were just empty boxes, but at that moment, it didn't matter. I was immersed in a serene and truly magical moment. I looked at my sister, standing on the other side of the fireplace, and I began to tell her something. Instantly, my fantasy bubble burst, as I heard, "Alright. Quiet. In 5, 4, 3 ... "

We knew what to do. The orchestra swelled as the lights came up, and Candie and I started busying ourselves with the task of decorating a hearth that was already fully decorated. I was amused, wondering if I looked as awkward as I felt. Why couldn't I have gotten the part of just playing with a toy under the tree? But I never had time to answer myself, because, at that moment, I heard applause, and saw Jonathan Winters walk onstage with his staff and Viking hat. He then said to us, "Come on over here, kids. I want to tell you a story." Following directions, we all stopped what we were doing, and headed to the couch ... except for one of us. My 4-year-old cousin Robbie decided he'd rather stay by the Christmas tree and play with the toys. Jonathan Winters was sitting there on the couch, beginning his tale. Most of my cousins were sitting down on the rug. However, I was sitting on the couch. I could see something going on out of the corner of my eye, lots of rustling and noise over by the tree. I couldn't tell exactly what he was doing, but from my vantage point, I could see it was Robbie running around behind us.

My Aunt Linda Lou, Robbie's mom, was frantically beckoning, and mouthing, "COME HERE!" but he appeared to be having too much fun. Then before anyone could stop him, Robbie picked up a large rubber ball under the tree, and hurled it straight at Jonathan Winters, knocking his Viking hat off as the cameras rolled. The audience began to laugh, and Mr. Winters seized the moment, going off-script. The rest of us had no idea what to do, but Winter's improvisation apparently was funnier than his original dialogue, so the director nodded and gave the crew a signal to keep rolling. The audience, director, and camera crew were laughing so hard, that some were wiping tears from their eyes. When this little impromptu sketch was over, my Aunt Linda Lou caught Robbie and held him on to him for the rest of the show. We did the musical singing part, and the show ended.

We all went backstage to wait for the next audience. But word came back, that the director had loved the unexpected improvisation so much, that he decided to just go ahead and use that take, making it unnecessary for us to do it again. We could all leave now. Robbie's mom was mortified, Robbie didn't seem to care, and all of us were irritated that we had to go home early without a second show.

Years later, Grandma ran into Jonathan Winters at another event. The first question out of his mouth was, "Hey Dale, how's that (blankity-blank) grandson of yours?" You know, I'm not sure Winters ever really let Rob off the hook for that. The funny part is, that Rob turned out to be a great human being, who sings with his lovely wife, Linda, pastors a church, and is hilariously funny. In all of our eyes, however, he will never live that down ... well ... that, and also the time he dropped a frozen turkey on Grandpa Roy's toe at Thanksgiving. But that's another story.

On the set of *The Dinah Shore Show* with my grandparents.

Jonathan Winters telling us a story. I am on the far right sitting next to Grandpa on the couch.

During these years they were very busy guest starring on variety and talk shows. In 1970, when they were enroute to do a guest appearance on the TV show, *Hee Haw*, they popped in at the Grand Ol' Opry in Nashville to sing a few songs for that show.

Chapter 19:

A TALE OF TWO GRANDMAS

There were no two grandmas more different than mine, in the history of ever. My mom's mom, Grandma Mabel, was a painfully shy individual, who wanted nothing more than to blend in with the paint on the wall. She wore jersey polyester dresses buttoned up to the neck, black chunky Grandma heels, you know, the kind that laced up, with thick, seamed stockings that cinched her calves in, making her knees bulge out like angry mackerels. But she was lots of fun too because she would make crafts with me. She was a kindergarten teacher in Hollywood where she lived. My friend, Bill Mumy, a child actor from *Lost in Space*, was in her class. I found it very odd that she always kept an open box of watercolors with a little paintbrush on her bathroom sink. I remember wondering why the color black seemed to be the only color she used, until I discovered her one morning, touching up her gray hair with it. What are my thoughts on this? Well, let's just say another piece of my somewhat peculiar life puzzle falls into place here. Oh, and by the way, she always smelled like talcum powder, and kept a daily stash of butterscotch balls in her purse.

Now my Grandma Dale was gregarious and friendly. She had a movie career, carried herself confidently, and never took "no" for an answer. She wasn't a stay-at-home grandma, but she was tons of fun. Her conversation was always current, her clothes always stylish, and you never knew what the day would hold when you were with her. She wore full skirts that cinched in at the waist with a wide belt, high heels, and usually some cat-eye sunglasses that she wore around her neck on some kind of beaded chain. She'd be wearing a jacket, but also carrying another one over her arm, along with a giant purse you could easily fit two or three cats in. To me, she was sort of like a boisterous Mary Poppins that created fun wherever she went. There were sure to be unlikely things happening when I tagged along with her.

Well, one day, when I was a sophomore in high school, Grandma Dale decided to take a plane trip from Los Angeles to come see us up in Los Gatos. She thought it would be fun to come up together with Grandma Mabel so she bought two plane tickets and called Grandma Mabel with the details. I would have liked to have heard my Grandma Mabel on the other end of the phone that day because I'm sure just the thought of traveling with this vociferous actress made her cringe with anxiety. Of course, she agreed to go because Grandma Dale was simply the hardest person ever to say no to.

The morning of their trip, they checked in at the terminal at LAX, grandma with her gaggle of suitcases, and Grandma Mabel clutching her purse, and one little overnight bag. On the way to the airport, Grandma Dale had decided they would probably get hungry on the plane because neither had gotten lunch yet. So she stopped at a fried chicken place and bought two box lunches to carry on to the plane. Grandma Dale boarded the plane with her carry-on, purse, extra jacket, hat, miscellaneous bag, and both box lunches. She was always helpful, and always in charge. I'm sure Mabel struggled to keep up with Dale's long strides through the airport. They boarded the plane, bumping and jostling their way down the aisle, to find their seats, stow their bags in the overhead bin, and buckle in. As they proceeded to get their box lunches laid out on their laps and prepare for take-off, the jetway retracted as the plane began to push back from the gate.

The captain came on and said, "Good afternoon, ladies and gentlemen. This is your Captain speaking and I'd like to welcome you to flight #853, headed to San Diego."

"SAN DIEGO?!!!" Grandma Dale shouted as she unbuckled herself and leaped out of her seat, sending her thigh and biscuits flying — of her chicken, that is.

"We can't go to San Diego! Come on, Mabel! Let's go! We've got to get off this plane!"

Yep. Here it was, the moment Grandma Mabel had dreaded, and with head down, mumbling something to look busy, Grandma Mabel dutifully unbuckled herself. The flight attendants rushed down the aisle to see what was the matter, as Grandma Dale was already gathering her things. Grandma Mabel still sat flustered in her seat, holding her drumstick. She would have preferred to just stay on the plane and fly to the wrong place instead of making a scene.

The flight attendants did their best to convince Grandma Dale to sit back down, but they were unsuccessful. Finally, one of the pilots in the cockpit got wind of this problem, so the plane rolled to a stop, and he personally walked back to settle the issue. After a meeting of the minds, the unsuccessful pilot walked back to the cockpit. They radioed the control tower and taxied back to the gate. The jetway was then moved back in place, and Grandma Dale, apologizing and explaining their predicament to the whole plane, quickly gathered up all of her belongings, and bustled back up the aisle with poor Mabel stuffing her chicken back in the box as she went.

They returned to the waiting area, and an airport employee escorted them over to the correct flight, which had been instructed to wait for them and was now delayed as well. The passengers on that plane stared them down silently, some even giving them the skunk-eye, as the two clearly mismatched grandmas found their new seats, and went through the whole process again of stowing their bags, and settling in.

The captain of this new plane got on the intercom and welcomed the passengers to flight #974 on its way to San Jose. He then paused, and added, "If there's anyone here who is NOT going to San Jose, I suggest you get off this plane right now!" Grandma Mabel was beyond mortified. Yet they both eventually made it to San Jose to tell us about it. I do believe, however, that was the last time they ever traveled together.

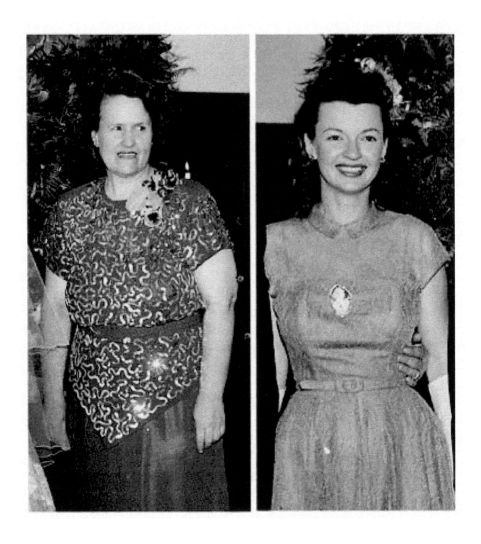

My two grandmas, Mabel (McCall) Campbell, and Dale Evans.

Chapter 20:

THE OLD AIRSTRIP

It was 1975. I was seventeen, a Junior in High School. My parents and I had driven down to Apple Valley for a visit with Grandma and Grandpa and some other family at their house on the highway for the weekend. After lunch Saturday, everyone was either napping or having small conversations here and there. I had just sat down in the family room to see what was on TV, when Grandpa popped his head around the corner, and whispered quietly, "You want to go for a ride?"

"Sure!" I answered as I jumped up. I asked my dad if it was alright and he nodded, so I grabbed my jacket.

I followed Grandpa out to the garage, where his motorcycle was parked. He reached for two helmets that were hanging on the wall and handed one to me.

"Ya gotta wear this," he said matter-of-factly, as he helped me tighten the strap of the helmet under my chin.

"I've never actually been on a motorcycle before!" I admitted under my breath.

"Well then, let's go!" he grinned.

He hopped on, turned the key, and suddenly the garage was filled with the roar of the engine. "Get on behind me, and put your arms around my waist," he shouted over his shoulder. I climbed on behind him, held on, and off we went.

We cruised down the frontage road and onto the highway there in Apple Valley. It was a beautiful day, and I could feel the sun warming my face while stopped at each traffic light. As we turned onto a side street, I couldn't help but smile. *I'm loving this!* I thought, gulping in mouthfuls of clean desert air while using grandpa's back as a bug shield. I leaned into the curves with him, just because it felt right, but not really knowing why, and he called over his shoulder to me that I was a "natural." Not understanding what that meant, I just kept hanging on.

We breezed through town until the traffic slowly faded into the background, and we were now galumphing along an old road in the desert, filled with cracks and potholes. Grandpa pointed out a few hawks along the way, and all around us was nothing but sand and Joshua trees. We turned and slowed to a stop, idling at the end of a very wide road that stretched as far as I could see.

"This is the old, deserted airstrip," he said. "They don't use it anymore and it's perfect for this. You ready?"

I hugged him tighter, took a deep breath, and nodded with a huge grin on my face. Knowing that Grandpa never attempted any sport halfway, I wasn't too surprised when we took off like a bullet. I'd seen him ride this fast on his horse, but never on a motorcycle, much less with me on the back of it. We absolutely flew on the old airstrip that day, up and down and up and down. "Wow! Again, Grandpa! Let's go again!" I leaned back laughing after every exhilarating pass to the other end. I'm not sure who had more fun that day, Grandpa Roy or me.

As the sun hovered low over the mountains, the air was getting a bit chilly. We decided it was probably time to head back. On the way home, the wind came up, and the air wasn't anything I wanted to gulp anymore, so I buried my face into his jacket and slipped my hands inside his warm pockets. I felt safe with him. Back at home, as we returned our helmets to their hooks on the wall, I felt happy. "Thank you, Grandpa! That was the most fun I've ever had!" I hugged him and opened the back door, as the warmth, and the smell of dinner cooking on the stove, made my world, at that moment, perfect.

On a different note, to say that my mom was displeased with my dad, for allowing me to go out on a motorcycle that day, would be an understatement. My dad was certainly in the "Chateau du Bow Wow" over that one. For me, however, no one could wipe that smile off my face. Not then, and not now.

Grandpa started riding bikes in the early 1930s when he couldn't afford a car or gas. Over the years, he was never without a bike in his garage. When he first came out to California, he would ride his motorcycle to Knotts Berry Farm when it was still just a berry farm, and he'd buy a pie for a nickel. My Uncle Dusty said he would sit there and have coffee and eat the whole pie.

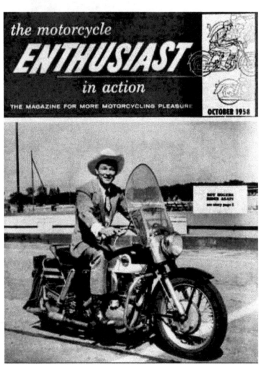

the motorcycle

ENTHUSIAST

in action

THE MAGAZINE FOR MORE MOTORCYCLING PLEASURE

OCTOBER 1958

Chapter 21:

SHE HAD NO IDEA

As we all started moving into our teen years, the number of grandchildren kept growing, to sixteen actually. Ten granddaughters and six grandsons. Through the late '60s, and '70s, Grandma and Grandpa were still very much in demand doing TV specials and personal appearances. They sometimes took us with them when they taped TV shows, and we'd sit in the audience up front. Their schedule was always filled with personal appearances.

In 1977, my Uncle Dusty, who was a contractor, built a new two-story house for Grandma and Grandpa about a mile away from the Highway House. The best part about their place was that it was right on the golf course, so there was grass. It was green! The worst part was that Grandma Smith had died. I missed her. I was now in college, so occasionally, I would drive out and spend the weekend with Grandma and Grandpa, just to get a little break from dorm life. It was a huge house, and my Uncle Dusty had built it in the shape of a horseshoe. So, for the trek upstairs and around to the last bedroom, you almost needed snacks for the journey. Once inside the bedroom, it was like a sound booth. You could launch a rocket and no one would hear you. However, the smell of Grandma brewing coffee in the morning traveled faster than the speed of sound, so I used it as my alarm clock on these "get-away" weekends.

Grandma and I would sit at the kitchen table in our pajamas, drink coffee, and talk about this and that and everything in between. She was a great listener, and I grew even closer to her than my own mother during my college years. I think grandparents have a special role that parents are sometimes just not able to fill in the same way. Grandparents have lived a lot of life and can offer wisdom, without getting too close to the situation or personally involved. They've already parented our parents, and learned from what worked, and what didn't, which is why they can be such great sounding boards. I could tell her anything with complete confidence that she would not be judgmental or critical. I knew there was nothing I could ever say that would change her fierce love for me. Grandma had either seen it, said it, or done it herself. She was my safe zone. Her memory was impeccable. She would remember all of the details of things I would share with her. When I'd see her the next time, she would just pick up where we left off from our last conversation, even asking about my roommates, Erin and Jodee, by name. She was amazing. I always enjoyed listening to her stories, or whatever her plans were for that day. She could read the phone book to me, and make it sound riveting.

One morning when I was there, she was sitting on the couch working on a crossword puzzle. She was stumped over an answer, and it was frustrating her. She couldn't put the book down until she solved it. I got up to get some coffee in the kitchen and as I was pulling a mug out of the cupboard, she suddenly let out a howl, "Oh my stars! It's ME! 47 down: D-A-L-E- E-V-A-N-S."

I shook my head and laughed. She was hilarious. Little known fact, however, she used to say that Grandpa was without a doubt the funniest person she knew. But she couldn't print half of the things he would whisper to her because it only made sense to the two of them. I guess that will forever be kept a secret. They were quite a pair.

This morning, Grandma was planning to take an old dress over to her little seamstress, for a sort of a "glamour makeover" for an upcoming guest appearance on television. Between 1965 and 1990, they had been on just about every variety and talk show there was; Barbara Mandrell, Carol Burnett, Bob Hope, Andy Williams, Dean Martin, John Davidson, Johnny Carson, David Letterman, *Good Morning America*, Tony Orlando, *The Muppet Show*, *Hee Haw*, and the list goes on. Even now, years after their passing, Grandma and Grandpa's voices can still be heard on the movie soundtracks of *Sleepless in Seattle*, and *Men in Black 3*. So now here in their 60s, they were still working, yet they were very frugal. She would choose a dress she already had, and ask her tailor to just add some rows of sequins, or outline a design on the front with rhinestones to make it "pop" and show up a little better for the TV cameras. She mixed and matched, cut and pieced, every which way but sideways to achieve the proper outfit, without spending any more money on herself.

However, the siren would always go off in my head, any time, she would turn her attention to me and utter the words, "Julie, I have something I think would look really good on you back in my closet. Come here." Immediately my brain would signal, *Mayday! Mayday! Abort! Abort!* Whatever it was, it was almost always something horrifyingly hideous. An Army bomber jacket embroidered with Dale Evans on the front AND back. A two-piece black velvet skirt and top, adorned with silver and gold metallic rick-rack from the '60s, or a long, pink, sequined dress that fit like a mermaid, with a chiffon wrap attached, that was so long, you could fling it around your neck, and whip six other people in the eye while doing so. I would always accept whatever it was with gratitude, while I would wonder inside, *What am I going to do with this?* I usually tucked them away in our Halloween costume boxes. Then later, I would see a clip of them on some previous television show, and lo and behold, she would be wearing that same outfit she had just given me. Then out of curiosity, I would usually dig it out of my Halloween box, hold it up, and say to myself, "Huh, Look at that! It's the same outfit," before putting it back in the box. Fortunately, I kept all of those hand-me-downs, and years later, I started making a hobby out of trying to find pictures of her wearing those outfits, to put inside the box with them.

At breakfast, she told me she needed help cleaning out the storage area. She asked me to go organize and bag up anything that could go to the Salvation Army to donate. So I got dressed, climbed up to the attic, and slowly opened the door. It smelled musty. The sun was shining and it was already uncomfortably hot up there. A beam of light shone down from the window, scattering the dust particles that were suspended in the air, which was stuffy and still. As I wound my way through the maze of boxes, there were clothes, shoes, files, and old letters. I found two big empty boxes to fill and began sifting through the items to find suitable donations. I found sweet letters to them from my Uncle Sandy, who had been in the Army over in Germany. Noticing the dates, I knew these were written shortly before he died. That sidetracked me for a while, but I left those safely in the box, for that was not part of my task.

When the boxes for the Salvation Army were filled with clothes and household items, I noticed two pairs of women's leather cowboy boots that were obviously very worn and scuffed. One pair was brown with gold stars on the fronts, heavily creased, with some areas cracked and faded from the sun, and the other pair, a navy blue, and not quite as worn, but with lots of stitching. Both had embroidered bootstraps that read, "Dale Evans." I ran my hands over the brown ones and held them to my nose to smell the worn leather. I could tell that these dusty, old boots were once strikingly beautiful because I had seen enough episodes of their '50s TV show to know that these were her work boots. *Lots of history behind these. If boots could only talk*, I thought to myself.

As I sat there on the attic floor, I pondered the fact that my grandparents had already lived an extraordinary life, right in front of my eyes all these years. Yet I was too busy growing up to notice until now. I finished up the rest of my organization and brought the two boxes down, carrying the boots on top. I slipped through the sliding glass door into the cool air again and plopped the boxes down by the door. Then I asked, "Grandma, do you really want these boots to go to the Salvation Army?"

Her answer was an unwavering, "Yes." I asked her very tentatively if maybe I could keep a pair of boots because they had so much history to them.

"You want those old things?" she responded.

"Yeah!" I grinned.

"Sure, Honey. But make sure the other pair is donated because I know there are people out there that need shoes!"

"Absolutely." I smiled. She was truly unaware, wasn't she?

As I drove back to college that weekend, I glanced over at her boots that I had carefully placed beside me in the front seat. I thought of the other boots that got donated that day, and I smiled, because someone, somewhere, who quite possibly was in desperate need of shoes, was going to be walking around wearing a pair of Dale Evans' cowgirl boots. They even said so ... on the bootstraps.

Visiting the old house fifteen years later when it happened to be up for sale again. The attic I cleaned out for her that day is that window upstairs on the far right.

Grandma wearing these boots on their weekly TV.

Grandma Dale wore this gown with grace. Then she gave it to me saying, it would fit me beautifully. Liar, Liar pants on fire, Grandma. I wrestle it like a wild boar every time I put it on, and I feel like a sequined sausage wearing it. I just wish you were here to laugh about it with me.

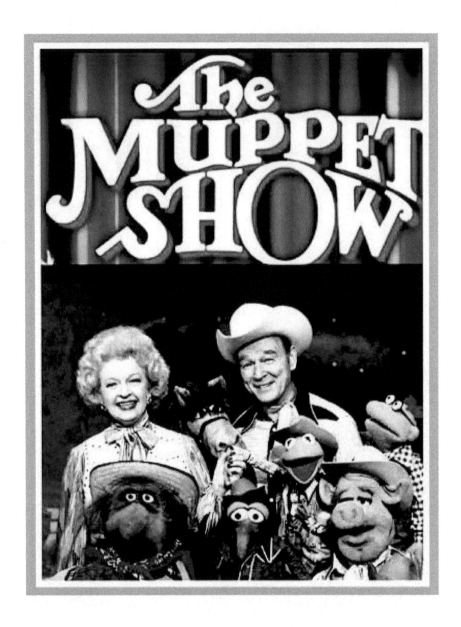

My grandparents on *The Muppet Show*. Original air date: May 17, 1979.

Chapter 22:

THE SWAP MEET

Occasionally, in college, when I would stay at their house, Grandma and I would be sitting at the kitchen table, and Grandpa would saunter in, wearing his robe and slippers. But on most days, he was already dressed, and asking if I wanted to get my clothes on, and go over to the museum with him so he could "Play ol' Roy," as he called it. It was his way of giving back to his fans. He knew how much it meant to people to be able to meet and greet and take pictures with him. He would always say, "If it weren't for the fans, there'd be no Roy Rogers." But secretly, I know he loved doing it, too. He'd get such a kick out of surprising people at the museum. One time I stood back and watched as he quietly stepped up behind a couple who were looking at one of the displays, and he joined in their conversation over their shoulders. They just about fell over when they turned around and saw Roy, himself, standing there with them. He loved doing that.

But this weekend, he asked me to go to the swap meet with him instead. I always looked forward to this, because he would dress incognito, wearing a baseball hat with dark glasses, and tennis shoes. We would meander past the tables, sticking closer to the center of the aisle. He would spy some knickknack he wanted, and then step to the side and inconspicuously point it out to me. We had it down. He would hand me a couple of bills, and tell me to talk the seller down to a price that he wanted to pay. If the seller wouldn't do it, I would walk. Grandpa lived through the depression when money was scarce. He was frugal. He taught his children (my aunts and uncles), as well as even us grandchildren, the value of a dollar, and how he worked hard for it. I don't know how many times he told me the story of the Christmas when he was a little boy, and his parents gave him a Barlow knife. That was the only thing they could afford to buy him for Christmas, and he was ecstatic! Well, that very day, he lost the knife and was devastated. Their family was poor, and he did not get another one. Grandpa never forgot that. He appreciated the little things and loved to find a bargain.

On this day, he was interested in a mirror framed with a leather ox harness. He quietly leaned over, slipped me some money, and mumbled how high he would go, then nonchalantly turned and walked a few steps away, looking at another table. I went up to the vendor and began chatting. The price was right, so I paid. But as our conversation continued, the vendor lowered his voice and shared an insider's secret.

"You know, sometimes Roy Rogers even makes it out to the swap meet!"

I courteously asked who Roy Rogers was, and to my surprise, the man gave me a quick education on my grandfather. "Wow!" I said. "He sounds like an amazing person! Have you ever met or talked to any of the others in the Rogers family?" He said he had not. But I smiled, thanked him, and left with Grandpa's mirror.

We continued strolling through the aisles until we came upon a vendor selling purses. "Oh! I got to show you these purses! They have pockets everywhere! Ya need a purse?" Grandpa asked eagerly. Before I could answer, he continued, "Here, I'll get you one of these. It has a place for everything!" The excitement in his voice and his squinty-eyed smile melted my heart, and though I didn't really need a purse, I walked away from the vendor with one. We carried our treasures back to the van. We rode in contented silence on the way back to the house.

"So what do you do with all this stuff you get at the swap meet, Grandpa?" I finally asked.

"Well," he said, "I usually get that look from Ma, ya know? And then I put it out in the garage.

I laughed. But when we got home, sure enough. He was right. Grandma was making lunch in the kitchen, and when she saw the huge mirror, she planted her hands on her hips, and exclaimed, "My stars, Papa! Where are you going to put THAT?"

"You called it, Grandpa!" I laughed. As I followed him out to his man cave.

Near the end of his life, he got into this endearing period of time when he kept buying these "sand pictures," as he called them, at the swap meet. They consisted of a wooden frame around two pieces of glass that had sand and different colored oil inside. When you turned them upside down, the sand would slowly trickle down, creating different landscapes. They all looked basically the same, but he was obsessed with them and kept buying more in different colors. Every morning, when he woke up, he would head straight to the dining room where he displayed them there on the window sill. He would meticulously turn every one of the eight frames upside down and watch the sand fall. Then he'd look around for anyone else in the room and ask, like an eager little kid, "Have you seen my sand pictures?" I'd say, "No, Grandpa, show me!" every time.

After he passed away, I was helping grandma clean out one of the closets downstairs, and I came across a box with all of his sand pictures. I was delighted for a quick second until I realized that they had all lost the oil inside, the sand was crusty, and they no longer worked. A wave of nostalgia swept over me, and I teared up, thinking of all of our visits to the swap meet. One by one, I placed the broken sand pictures into the black garbage bag. "It's just stuff," I reminded myself. I've got those memories.

One ox yoke mirror, $20, one leather purse, $40, eight sand pictures, $10 apiece, the fun we had haggling? Priceless.

The home that Uncle Dusty built for them on the golf course in Apple Valley, CA. This was their Christmas card photo that year, 1977.

Photo by Greg Vaughan

My college years 1976-1981.

During the same timeframe Grandpa guest starred on the *Wonder Woman* TV show in 1977.

Grandpa and I surveying and testing the fruit in his "garden" out back.

Chapter 23:

NO ONE TELLS ME ANYTHING

I have run into many people over the years who know so much more about my family than I do — you know, facts, dates, careers, and general information. Growing up, no one really told me much about my grandparents or their unique job. I just watched, heard bits and pieces of conversations, and experienced things happening around me. To be fair, even if the adults had taken me aside, I wouldn't have paid much attention anyway. I was too busy running down the hall, playing with my cousins, or snitching another piece of Grandma's homemade pink and green taffy off the buffet. We were just grandchildren having fun.

One day I was sitting at my desk in my dorm room at college in 1978. My focus was on a paper that was due on Friday, but I had the radio on low as I worked. Unexpectedly, I heard the name, "Dale Evans" pop out, coming from the station. I turned up the volume just in time to catch the host saying that Dale Evans wrote that iconic song, "Happy Trails," for their television show.

"What??? Wait. She wrote that? No one ever told me that!" I said out loud, as I leaned back in my chair, to contemplate this travesty.

I immediately got up, walked over to the phone, and dialed Grandma's number because back in those days, we actually memorized people's phone numbers. She picked up the phone on the other end, and before she could even get out a "Hello," I started.

"Grandma! The guy on the radio just said you wrote that!"

"Wrote what?" she responded.

"Happy Trails!" I said in a bewildered tone.

There was a long pause ... "Well, yeah, I did. Why?"

"Why didn't you ever tell me?" I asked.

"Well Baby, I just didn't think it was that important, that's all."

"Seriously, Grandma?" I laughed. "Everyone knows that song. I'm 20 years old and I'm just now finding this out from some guy on KRLA am radio, that my own grandma wrote that? Stink! No one in this family tells me anything."

She laughed, and said, "Julie, you are a pistol!" We talked for a bit, and she explained how she had written that song one day, in about three hours, because she thought Grandpa should have his own theme song to close every show. She wanted it to be western sounding, so she modeled the chorus after the cowboys who would whistle going down the trail into the Grand Canyon and then would wait to hear the trail boss at the bottom whistle back. She wanted the words to symbolize riding the trail of life, no matter what comes your way. Some trails are happy. Some aren't. The song was released in 1952 and became one of the top 100 western songs of all time.

We talked about how biographical the words to that song had become, in summing up their life, after losing three of their children and having so many heartaches along with their happiness. But she reminded me, "Honey, God is good, all the time!" When I hung up the phone, I couldn't help but smile. That's the kind of people they were grateful and unassuming, but not boastful about it. She really didn't think it was that important. I loved that about them. They never pushed "their story" on you. It's still true today. My Aunt Cheryl, Uncle Dusty, Aunt Linda Lou, and Aunt Dodie are now the only siblings left after Aunt Mimi died last year. They all have a wealth of fantastic stories, but they don't just assume you want to hear them. You have to sit down and ask. You have to take the initiative. I've learned to do that, because otherwise, as I've said ...

No one in this family tells me anything!

"HAPPY TRAILS"

Written by Dale Evans in 1952

Some Trails are happy ones,
Others are blue
It's the way you ride the trail that counts
Here's a happy one for you.

CHORUS
Happy trails to you, until we meet again.
Happy trails to you, keep smilin' until then.
Who cares about the clouds when we're together?
Just sing a song and bring the sunny weather.
Happy trails to you, 'til we meet again.

10 TRIVIA FACTS ABOUT "HAPPY TRAILS"

When Dale wrote the song, "Happy Trails," she scribbled the words on an envelope she had in her purse, and taught those lyrics to Roy just minutes before they were to sing it on the air for the first time.

Van Halen would often use "Happy Trails" as their show closer.

Janis Joplin recorded "Happy Trails" as a birthday greeting for her friend, John Lennon, three days before her death in 1970.

"Happy Trails" was featured in the movie *28 Days* in 2002, starring Sandra Bullock.

John Stamos and Dave Coulier sing "Happy Trails" in the Season 4 *Full House* episode, "Danny in Charge."

The song "Happy Trails" was inducted into the Grammy Hall of Fame in 2008.

The Reagan Administration used the song "Happy Trails" at the White House when he left the presidency in 1989.

The XIX Olympic Winter Games in Salt Lake City, Utah ended the closing ceremony with the children leading the whole stadium of 50,000 people in "Happy Trails."

In 2010, the Western Writers of America named "Happy Trails" one of the top 100 western songs of all time.

My grandma wrote that song.

Chapter 24:

THE TALKERS CLUB

Grandma called me on the phone at college, pretty regularly. Grandpa hated talking on the phone because he was horrible at small talk and chit-chat. He was always that way. Early on, in his career, the Republic executives wanted him to go to more Hollywood parties so he could mingle more and be seen with other celebrities. "It'll be good for your career!" they said. But that just wasn't for Grandpa, who said he always felt like the shy kid from Duck Run, who would stare at his feet and not know what to say. He finally struck a deal, asking if he could bring a friend. "Sure!" they replied. So at the next party, he brought a couple of his hunting buddies. They sat on the couch all evening and talked about coon hunting. Needless to say, the studio quit asking him to go.

He was a man of few words. Even during big family gatherings for Thanksgiving at their house, he would slip away to the bedroom once in a while, for some alone time away from the din of the "crowd," even though it was just family. Once, two guys came in the back door and mingled nonchalantly through our group of about fifty, taking a small plastic plate and something to eat, as several of us whispered, "Do you know who that is?" When they got around by the front door, Grandpa looked them up and down and asked, "Who are you?" They were stunned and didn't know what to say. "Happy Trails!" Grandpa replied as he opened the front door, and ushered them out.

One morning when we were sitting around their breakfast table, Grandpa turned to me with a glint of humor and said, "You know? I think you might be the newest member of the Talker's Club." Grandma laughed, but then shook her head solemnly, pointed her finger at me, as she often did when she was about to say something really important, and she said, "Ohhhh Baby, your personality, the way you are, is more like me than anyone else in the family. You know what I mean?" I just smiled. I was never quite sure if that was good or bad, and I never asked, and she did tell me that on more than one occasion. Then years later, while sitting at the dinner table at my house, Uncle Dusty told me the same thing. So you know what? I'll take it. Here is my conclusion. If I do ever remind people of someone else, I guess it might as well be Grandma. We were truly kindred spirits.

Chapter 25:

THE SCOTLAND TRIP

I don't know if you've ever taken a trip with Dale Evans, but I did, several times actually, and I lived each time to tell about it. In the summer of '81, my mom, dad, my childhood friend Sherilyn, and I took a trip to the British Isles. Our family roots are in Scotland and Ireland. My dad had always wanted to meet Willy Merrilees, the retired Chief Constable of Scotland Yard. Mr. Merrilees also oversaw the orphanage there in Edinburgh where my Aunt Mimi had lived until she was thirteen, at which point she was brought over by my grandparents as a foster child. When Grandma heard of our plans, she immediately expressed interest in coming along. "Absolutely!" my dad said. August came and the five of us were Scotland bound.

I'll skip over the part where my dad rented the tiniest compact car on the face of the planet. On second thought, I'll give you every detail. It was the size of a roller skate and should have come with a wind-up key. My parents sat in the front, and the three of us (Sherilyn, me, and Grandma) sat in the rear. The back seat had enough room to seat a couple of squirrels comfortably. But we poured ourselves in, filling every inch of space in that backseat. Once we put our purses on the floor, we had to wait until we got out of the car to be able to reach them again, and when the doors did open, we all popped out like a busted can of biscuits.

Now my dad, in his thoughtful foresight, had called the Glasgow rent-a-car company ahead of time. He had meticulously asked for the car's trunk measurements and then had carefully measured each piece of our luggage back at home. He had confidently assured us that all of our suitcases would fit like a glove inside the trunk. Unfortunately, his measurements were off by just a tad and they didn't all fit. So we had to take turns holding one of the suitcases on our laps in the backseat throughout the whole trip. Make no mistake. It did not ruin the trip. It just added to the pain in our sides from laughing. "We're OFF ... like a dirty shirt!" my dad proudly announced, for the first time, as our little tuna can lurched forward out of the rental lot, and off we went, our faces pressed against the side windows.

We sailed along quite nicely on the "wrong" side of the road with the steering wheel on the right, which was weird for all of us to get used to. My grandma was a self-professing backseat driver under the best of circumstances, so my dad never lacked for driving tips and directions. Like clockwork, Grandma could be heard interjecting, "Tom! Tom! You going to use those brakes?" as she mashed her foot on her imaginary brake on the floor of the backseat while gripping my shoulder.

During one of our many conversations along the journey, Grandma told us that on one of her trips to the Holy Land, her guide had informed her that people could easily pick out the tourists to pickpocket. He had warned her to beware, keeping her belongings close, especially her purse. So all through the countryside of Scotland, which was not exactly a hotbed of purse-snatchers, she wore her purse around her neck like a feedbag.

Scotland was quite picturesque with views of green meadows, low rock walls, thatched roofs, and grazing sheep. We stopped a lot to take photos. However, Grandma seized most of her opportunities to capture the countryside, as we were driving. Not wanting to ask my dad to make a special photo stop just for her, she just snapped them straight out the side window as we sped along, which made for some impressionistic photos. Sherilyn and I shook our heads. Fortunately, I grew up with Sherilyn, and she had known Grandma for a long time, so no explanation was needed.

We stopped the next day at St. Andrews, the oldest golf course in the world. Since its inception, St. Andrews has been for "Men Only." No women had ever been allowed to enter the clubhouse before our visit. Well, the gentleman who greeted us to show us around, knew Chief Constable Merrilees and was a huge Roy Rogers fan, so he snuck all of us into the "Gentlemen Only" private clubhouse to take a look around. There was a fire in the large stone fireplace and stained-glass windows on all sides, lots of dark wood and books. I was sort of expecting Sherlock Holmes, smoking his pipe, to slowly peer around the wingback chair in the corner. It was fascinating looking at all of the old paintings on the walls. But then we heard footsteps, and we were quickly ushered out the back door. We journeyed on to the woolen mill.

After one of our overnight stays, and shortly after we had taken off in the car for the next town, my dad realized he needed some travel information in his briefcase. We stopped on the side of a beautiful tree-lined road. He hoisted his briefcase onto the roof of the car, propping it open while he rummaged through his files. After retrieving the necessary documents, he got back in the car with them. Not even a minute down the road, we all heard a strange flup ... flup ... flup-flup sound, and it seemed to be coming from above and behind. Sherilyn and I turned around to look out the back window, just in time to see a long trail of papers floating behind us, as more papers continued sailing off the top of the car. "Stop! Your briefcase!" I blurted. He pulled over, and we all piled out of the car, spending the next 20 minutes retrieving the contents of the briefcase, along this lovely country road. I suppose then, that it was not unusual that cars coming upon the scene, would slow down, and inch along, peering curiously out their windows at this unlikely group of road workers.

When we got to the next hotel, the adults were all pretty exhausted, so we ate and they went to bed early. But before they retired to their rooms, a crazy idea popped into my head.

"Hey!" I said to Sherilyn. "Let's borrow the two wigs Grandma brought, put 'em on, and go take ridiculous pictures of ourselves around the hotel!"

Sherilyn was always game for anything, and Grandma was too tired to care, so we took off about midnight each wearing a different wig, in search of what is now known as some "insta-gram-able spots." I'd like to think we were ahead of our time.

Later that night, after we had gone back to our own room, the hotel had a late check-in arrival. Unbeknownst to Grandma, one of the hotel staff had accidentally rented her room out twice. Sometime in the middle of the night, two nice men, sporting full beards, wearing long robes and turbans, and chatting very loudly and happily in another language, turned the key and swung open her door. When they flipped on the light, they were immediately startled, letting out a surprised yell, which woke her up, causing her to answer with a startled shout, as she sat up straight in bed. The men began bowing, backing nervously out into the hallway, exclaiming, "Saluta! Saluta!" Grandma responded, "Well, Saluta to you too!" Then she rolled over and went back to sleep.

The next morning when she told us about it, she just shrugged. However, the hotel front desk clerk felt awful and apologized profusely for double-booking the room. Grandma just took it in stride. I hope the two gentlemen eventually thought it was as funny as we did. I looked for them down in the lobby the next morning but to no avail.

We packed up and loaded the car. As I stood waiting to be seated with Grandma at the bottom of the stairs in the breakfast room, my dad walked by, mentioning to us quietly under his breath, that we needed to get some bran flakes for Sherilyn, who had a little travel constipation thing going on. Hearing that, Grandma turned and saw Sherilyn descending the staircase, and she bellowed, in front of everyone in the breakfast room, "What? Sherilyn? You're constipated?"

"Ahhh, there it is." I turned, stifling a laugh. The oblivious "I-Don't-Know-How-Loud-I-Really-Am!" voice, at its finest. Sherilyn and I, to this day, still talk about that one.

You know, we did finally get some bran, and we did finally reach Edinburgh. We were welcomed into the home of Mr. Merrilees in his Scottish kilt and knee socks, and his lovely wife, Roberta. Mr. Merrilees (or "Uncle Willie" as my Aunt Mimi used to call him), sat by the fire that foggy, damp evening, telling us stories about his years in charge of Scotland Yard, and all about when he and my grandparents met the Queen of England while they were there on a rodeo tour. He spoke lovingly of Aunt Mimi and her life there in the orphanage, before she went to America, to live permanently with my grandparents. The next evening, he and Roberta took us to the famed Royal Edinburgh Military Tattoo Ceremony at the castle on the hill.

The term "tattoo" actually comes from the 17th-century Dutch phrase, "doe den tap toe," which means "turn off the tap," a signal to tavern owners each night played by a drum corps signaling the soldiers to stop drinking, and retire for the evening. Then, in the 18th-century, the term "tattoo" was used to describe the last duty call of the day. After that, it then developed into a ceremonial form of evening entertainment performed by military musicians, and today, it is performed annually at the castle in Edinburgh by British Armed Forces, Commonwealth, and international military bands. This prestigious festival is held every year in August.

We were fortunate enough to be able to sit front and center with Mr. Merrilees in his private box for the ceremony, during which the whole stadium stood up and saluted him during the opening fanfare. We watched an unparalleled performance that night, of Scottish dancing, bagpipe bands, and pageantry against the backdrop of the majestic 15th-century Castle Esplanade. It was an event I will never forget.

Even though the whole point of this story was to get to Edinburgh, I do tend to spend more time on the silly things that happen along the way. But when you think about it, isn't most of life about the daily details? My Texas cousins, Melinda and Melodie, whose grandma was my Grandma Dale's cousin, once told me, that a trip is as much about enjoying the journey as it is arriving at the destination. I believe that. I continue to take their wise words to heart, and our wonky Scotland trip really does remain in my memories, as one of the best trips ever.

Just make sure if you ever go ... pack light, and rent a bigger car.

One of our "insta-gram-able" moments in Scotland with two of
Grandma's wigs.

Grandma with former Chief-Constable of Scotland Yard, Willie Merrilees and his wife, Roberta, at their home in Edinburgh. My Aunt Mimi knew him from the orphanage when she was young as "Uncle Willie."

On our way up to the castle in Edinburgh that evening to attend the
Royal Military Tattoo with the Merrilees.

Chapter 26:

199 CLAY PIGEONS

"So, what do you want for graduation?" Grandma asked. I was graduating in three short weeks with a B.A. and teaching credential from Biola University in Southern California. I had no brain space to think of anything other than finishing up my last few finals. Not knowing how to answer her, I asked if I could think about it. "Sure," she said, "and Honey, Grandpa and I are really proud of you." That felt good.

After thinking about it for a few days, I decided I didn't really want or need anything. But knowing how much I loved spending time with them, I got back to her with my answer. "I'd like to go pheasant hunting with Grandpa. Then I'd love it if you would cook it up. Then my roommates and I could pick a night to come over and we can all have dinner."

From the sound of her response, it was obvious that she was not expecting that request. Nonetheless, she sounded very pleased and said that Grandpa would be thrilled.

The next day, Grandpa called me, which was remarkable in itself, because, as you now know, he hated talking on the phone. In fact, when I would call the house, if he answered, I would often make a game out of seeing how long I could keep him on the phone, before he would say the words, "Here, let me get Ma." He told me he was looking forward to it, and that he wanted me to come out the next weekend to practice shooting clay pigeons with him at the ranch. Then we would set up the time to go to the Pheasant Club.

So it was set. We had a date for target shooting. I drove out to spend the weekend with them. Saturday morning I slept in. When I shuffled downstairs to the kitchen in my pajamas, both Grandma and Grandpa were sitting at the table talking about schedules, while Grandma scrawled a note on her napkin. She wrote on anything she could find, even when writing her books. She was always on the run, so often there would be napkins, post-it notes, spiral notepaper, and used envelopes that she would keep, stuffed in her purse, that held everything from her grocery list to the ideas for her next book.

"Howd'ja sleep, Sugarfoot?" Grandma smiled, as she fixed her gaze on me while drumming her fingers on the table, a little habit she picked up later in life.

I always slept well out at their house in Apple Valley because it was so quiet. "My head hit the pillow and I was out like a carp," I answered.

"Well, why don't we go in about an hour," Grandpa said. "I've got to stop by the museum first."

Grandma got up, walked into the living room, and sat down at the piano. "Whatcha doin'?" I asked as I followed her.

"Ohhhh it's just a little secret I have planned for you!" she winked. "You'd better get dressed. You know Grandpa likes to get over to the museum early." I was dumbfounded and had no idea what she was talking about. But I went upstairs, dressed, and began my day.

About a year later, when I got married, she and Grandpa sat on the piano bench at our reception and sang a personalized version of "Happy Trails," that she had written for us. Then she sang another song she had written just for me, simply called, "Julie." *So that's the secret she was working on!?*

I get teary even now when I think back on it. I saved the paper with the words to the song she had written. Of course, you can barely read her chicken-scratch handwriting. But how precious it was to receive that unique gift.

Getting back to the task at hand, Grandpa and I left that day for the museum. Inside the back door, he motioned for me to follow him, as we wound around the glass cases filled with memories of their lives. I passed the family Bible, that was always in a prominent place in their home, the lion rug that I used to lie on, and even Grandpa's rock collection, that was missing the cherished ones he had given me that wonderful day when I was nine. I smiled, thinking back to those days. All of the rhinestone show-clothes that I would sneak in to peek at in their closet, were proudly hanging there for all to see now. Passing Trigger and Bullet, I thought of how much I had loved their dogs over the years, and the time Grandpa had set me on top of Trigger to step back with my dad and take my picture. Then we came to the gun case. He unlocked the glass door, stepped in, and reached for the rifle on the wall that was labeled, "The gun from Clark Gable." He chuckled and said quietly, "Here. I want you to use this gun today and I'll tell you the story about it when we get in the car." I loved his stories. We walked back through the gift shop, saying good morning to Cleda, his older sister, who often worked at the museum, and then hopped in the car.

"So about that rifle I pulled out of the case for you this morning," he began ...

Back in the '60s when Grandma and Grandpa lived at the ranch in Chatsworth, Clark Gable, and a few other Hollywood guys came out to the skeet shooting range. Well, "Old Clark," as Grandpa called him, had just gotten a new hand-carved Winchester shotgun, which he shot miserably with that day. As he walked back to the clubhouse with Grandpa, he was so angry about missing the targets so many times, that he fumed, "Does anybody want to buy this (blankity-blank) gun?" Well, Grandpa said he thought it was "mighty pretty," so he told Clark he'd buy it from him. And he did. Grandpa grinned, and added, "a few months later, I went to the big trap and skeet match in Ohio and shot 199 out of 200 with that gun! Best gun I ever bought!" We laughed. But the truth of it was, that Grandpa was an amazing marksman. Not many people ever beat him ... no matter what gun he used.

We pulled around behind the barn at the ranch and got out. He lifted the box of yellow clay pigeons from the back seat and got me all set up to do some target practice. He gave me a quick safety lesson, a rundown of the gun parts, and helped me get my stance. Then he stepped back and said, "Now you get all nice and ready with the gun on your shoulder and when you're ready, you say, *Pull!* Then I'll fire it off and you aim and pull the trigger. You think ya got it?"

"You know it, Grandpa," I said. "Pull!"

Well, we went through the entire box of clay disks that morning. I had the same stats as Grandpa had that day with the Gable gun in Ohio when he shot 199 out of 200, with only one slight difference. I MISSED 199 out of 200 of those annoying little yellow disks. Dejected, I climbed back into the truck with him. "I'm sorry I wasted all of your clay pigeons, Grandpa."

I looked down at the floor and then back over at him. He was smiling, but shyly looking straight ahead with those squinty, kind eyes. "No," he said. "It wasn't a waste at all." "You know," he continued awkwardly, "when you were young and used to run from me when I was in that neck brace, I thought you'd never want anything to do with me again. I'm just happy you grew out of that, and you want to spend some time with your old grandpa."

I knew two things in that moment. First, I couldn't hit a clay pigeon even if it was strapped to the barrel end of my gun, but most importantly second, I had a grandpa who, even though I knew it was hard for him to do, had just opened up, and shared his feelings. In that moment, who cared about clay pigeons?

Chapter 27:

PHEASANT HUNTING WITH GRANDPA

The day had arrived to go pheasant hunting with Grandpa. We were to meet Saturday morning, at 8 a.m. *sharp* in Ontario, just off the Highland exit. I would then follow him to the gun club just a few miles away. He couldn't stand it when people were late, so I left Anaheim in plenty of time to be a few minutes early. There were no other cars around so as I exited, I noticed him right away parked on the shoulder of the exit ramp. I pulled up next to him and rolled my window down.

"Wow!" he exclaimed. "You're on time and even early."

"You seem so surprised!" I laughed.

He waved for me to follow him, as he pulled out in front of me. At the gun club, I parked and walked over to his van as he opened up the back, and began taking things out. "Here you go," he said, handing a backpack vest to me. "Try putting this on and see if it fits."

"What am I going to need this big pocket for?" I asked.

"To keep your bird in," he said matter-of-factly.

"Wait. What? Did you say my bird?"

"Yup. The one you're going to get today," he said grinning, as he walked away toward the already sunbaked field.

It was going to be a scorcher. I stood there a second, pondering what he had just said, and wondering if it was too late to back out. But I zipped up my vest and hurried to catch up with him.

"Where are the birds?" I asked. He didn't answer at first. But as we neared the field, he dropped his voice to a whisper. He told me the birds were all around, but we would have to wait 'til one flushes. "Flushes?" I whispered. At that moment, I wished that I had read up on some of the morning's terminology. It was like I was a visitor in a foreign land, and he was speaking another language. I was still contemplating what kind of bird you would have to be in order to flush when his buddy quietly appeared beside us. Pleasantries were exchanged, and then we all waited in silence, sometimes trekking through the brush to find a different spot. Grandpa looked over at me and beckoned me to head left with him. Then we stopped, stood still, and listened. The whole world seemed to pause, except for the distracting bead of sweat that was rolling down my forehead. "No wonder he loves going hunting," I thought as we waited in silence. "He doesn't have to worry about making small talk."

All of a sudden, there was a flurry of flapping, and my heart jumped. The pheasant flew out of the bushes about 50 feet in front of us. "That's it! Get 'em!" Grandpa whispered excitedly. I raised my Clark Gable shotgun, aimed, and fired. It sort of sounded like my gun fired twice, and the pheasant dropped out of the sky. I froze.

"Did you hear that?" I whispered breathlessly.

"Hear what?" Grandpa asked.

"My gun. I think it fired twice. Did I get him?"

"You sure did!" he exclaimed, as he congratulated me.

I stopped. He was a little too excited, and not as surprised as he should have been. My eyes narrowed, and I stepped back to study his face, which was now showing signs of contradiction.

"Wait a minute. That was you! I must have missed, so you got him, huh!"

He was now grinning like some mischievous kid, caught in the middle of a prank. "Ohh for shame, Grandpa! You were telling me a big windy!"

"Well, I was just making sure, because you clipped his wing there, see? So I was just helping things out a little," he said, winking to his buddy. "Come on. Let's go get him."

Well, sure enough, Grandpa picked up that dead bird and stuffed him in the backpack vest I was wearing. "I was afraid you were going to do that," I said, wrinkling my nose at the thought of tromping around in the hot sun, carrying a dead bird on my back. But we kept looking and listening. My mind began to wander, and I wondered why he hadn't brought his bird dog, Sam. I figured it was probably because he didn't want me accidentally shooting his dog or something. We waited some more in the stillness. I noticed some gnats buzzing around my ears. I should've brought my camera, and maybe a bottle of water, I pondered. Suddenly, my thoughts were interrupted, when my backpack abruptly lurched with movement and frenzied flapping. I tried as best I could, not to scream, but I couldn't stop myself from frantically whispering, "IT'S ALIVE! IT'S STILL ALIVE!"

He thought that was pretty funny, and before I knew it, he had taken it out of my pack and done something to it, before stuffing it back in there. He told me later, when I was calm, that he had wrung the bird's neck to kill it instantly and humanely. "Oh, that makes me feel so much better!" I cringed.

Well, after each of us had gotten a bird, we headed back to the clubhouse, because Grandpa said he wanted to introduce me to his friends. As we entered, I immediately noticed that I was the only female amongst a lot of old guys. Grandpa put his arm around my shoulder, and proudly boasted, "Hey guys. This here is my granddaughter, Julie!" After a whole lot of friendly, gravelly voices greeted me, they all shared a few stories, and we headed out.

Just as we had planned, Grandma cooked the pheasant, and my roommates joined in. We sat around the table, laughing and telling stories.

Grandma shared with us that Grandpa took her coon hunting on their honeymoon. Yes, you read that right, on their honeymoon. She had gotten so mad at him for letting the dogs tree that innocent little animal, that Grandpa had quietly said, "I think it's probably best that I don't take you huntin' again."

"You got that right, Bub!" she had answered, storming off.

I'm pretty sure that I am on that same page as Grandma was. But I still wouldn't have traded that experience with my grandparents for any other graduation gift. It is a memory of time spent that I will hold in my heart for the rest of my life. Besides, we all had a lovely dinner of pheasant, roasted garlic potatoes, green beans, corn on the cob, fruit salad ... and ... well ok, maybe a tiny side of buckshot.

College graduation dinner with Grandma and Grandpa.

When I mentioned the day after hunting, that I wished I had gotten a photo of us, Grandpa pulled over to the side of the road, jumped out, and made me re-enact it. "Grandpa, you're so embarrassing."

Biola University Graduation 1981

We had 600 people at our wedding and I think 550 of them were there to see Roy and Dale. At the reception, Grandma and Grandpa made up a personalized version of "Happy Trails" and sang it directly to us. Then Grandma sat down at the piano and sang the special song she had written about me, simply called, "Julie." **Below** are the lyrics she scribbled on the back of a Barbara Mandrell Call Time Sheet. The words are also deciphered and typed beside it.

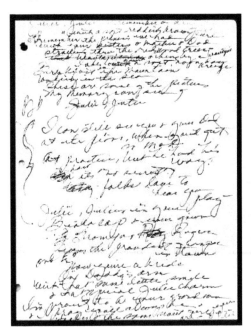

"Julie, Julie. I remember a dear little girl... just a soft, reddish brown curl. I remember the picnics we had with your sisters, and mother, and dad. Strolling through the redwood trees, and a home by a beautiful lake with a noonday breeze. Breakfast on the mountain, wading in the sea, these are some of the pictures my memory can see. Julie, Julie.

I can still see you and your dad at the piano, when you'd get so mad at practice, but he had his way. Now it's no secret, folks loved to hear you play.

Julie Julie in your Biola cap and gown. Grandpa was the proudest grandpa in town. Now you're a bride on daddy's arm, with that same little smile, and special Julie charm. I'm proud to be your grandma, and I pray you'll always be, happy and the same sweet girl you are... Julie."

Chapter 28:

THE FOX FAMILY SINGERS

My parents were both musicians. My dad, Tom, the oldest of the Rogers' siblings, lived with Grandma over by UCLA but was attending USC, when a guy named, Roy Rogers, entered the picture. Dad graduated with a Masters in Music Education, with an emphasis in flute. My mom's situation, however, was the exact opposite. She lived over by USC, but went to UCLA, graduating with a B.A. and a teaching credential in Physical Education. She was also a pianist/organist. For many years, there was good-natured rivalry during college football season at our house.

They met in high school when they both worked their first jobs at the Hollywood Bowl. My dad was an usher, and my mom sold programs. On warm summer nights, during the concerts, they would both hike up to the highest row of seats and enjoy Beethoven Symphonies, Mozart Concertos, and Tchaikovsky's sweeping melodies under the stars.

When they got married and had the three of us girls, it was natural for them to give us opportunities to take music lessons. We all played the piano and a stringed instrument from the time we were little. We also sang together as a family, and not just on camping trips. The five of us were called "The Fox Family Singers" and we were in high demand, performing for Grange meetings, convalescent homes, church conferences, and military bases. Ok, we weren't exactly Bob Hope and Raquel Welch, on a USO tour, but I have no doubt that we were entertaining, riding in with our fringed skirts on our stick horses, led by my dad, who was also all duded up with his cap gun and cowboy gear. How my parents got my two older sisters to keep putting themselves through this embarrassment, well into their teens, I will never know, because I was ready to ditch my stick horse when I reached fourth grade.

We sang Western music, some songs written by Grandma, and sacred music toward the end of the program. Usually, our shows went fairly smoothly. But one time at a Grange meeting, my dad thought he heard our cue, so we came galloping in, guns-a-blazing, only to find out, the man on the platform was just giving the announcements. He stared at my dad with a horrified look, as if we had just stormed the battlefront. Nothing worse than having to turn around, shamefully, carrying your stick horses back up the aisle, only to have to come roaring in on them again, ten minutes later. Amazingly, we didn't have a mutiny in our station wagon on the way home.

Singing with my family was not always embarrassing, however. We did perform with our grandparents at the Dorothy Chandelier Pavilion in Los Angeles. I was 6 years old, and there were no guns or stick horses involved. Inside the concert hall were 3,000 velvet seats, and a foyer lit with dazzling, crystal chandeliers. Out front, a whole row of magnificent fountains, greeted people as they strolled in for the concert, wearing their hats, furs, and fancy coats. I remember it vividly, with the most exhilarating part being the cheese and crackers we ate from my mom's purse backstage.

In 1972, during the summer after my eighth-grade year, again my family sang with Grandma and Grandpa for a Billy Graham Crusade at the Oakland Coliseum. Billy Graham and his wife, Ruth, were very dear friends of my grandparents for years. Grandma and Grandpa even flew over and brought Trigger to England for one of Billy's crusades. The Grahams were wonderful people, as genuine as they come. But meeting him that day was a little intimidating, as he was very tall, with piercing blue eyes. Definitely one of those people that's hard not to notice when they walk into a room.

We arrived early for a soundcheck. That's when I realized the place looks a lot bigger when you are standing down on the field, in the center of the turf. Billy Graham asked us, along with Cliff Barrows, George Beverly Shea, and my grandparents, to come down into the basement under the stadium for prayer before the meeting. As we filed in reverently, I noticed the small circle of metal folding chairs in the center of a dimly lit, cement room, that looked much like a small parking garage. We found our seats. It was silent for a minute, and then he spoke. "Whoever would like to pray, just speak it out if you feel so led." We all bowed our heads, and everything became completely still, as we all waited for that first person to lead out with a prayer. Meanwhile, I'm thinking, *Ok, I'm thirteen, sitting right next to Reverend Billy Graham. Pray out loud? Uhhh ... that will be a definite no-go for me.* So I sat there without making a peep. Mr. Graham ended our meeting with a prayer of his own. Then he spoke with Grandma and Grandpa about a few last-minute details. We all walked back out onto the field, this time in the stadium filled with 40,000 people, an army of ushers, and television boom cameras everywhere. The crusade was something I had definitely seen before, but never from the backside of Billy Graham's suit. We sang with my grandparents that evening, "It is No Secret" by Stuart Hamblen, (another family we have been long-time friends with), and all went well.

Later on in my life, when I was in my early 40s, my sisters and I were appearing around the country at different western festivals. We had the rare privilege of performing onstage in the Isaac Stern Auditorium at Carnegie Hall, in New York City, and also at The Grand Ole Opry in Nashville. Again, these were opportunities that were presented to us, only because of our family heritage. I didn't take them lightly then, and I certainly don't now.

My life has been a bit of a paradox, living on the edge of their spotlight. Sometimes I am Julie, Roy and Dale's granddaughter, but most of the time, I am Julie the school teacher, or Julie the soccer mom, or Julie the "fill-in-the-blank." I think my Uncle Dusty said it best when he said that Grandma and Grandpa were "ordinary people who lived extraordinary lives. Because of that, my life too has been a blend of the ordinary and the extraordinary" — *and I wouldn't change a thing.*

Fox Family singers in training.

Fox Family singers on stage with stick ponies.

On stage at the Grand Ole Opry

Billy Graham and his wife, Ruth, as well as Johnny and June Cash were longtime friends.

Chapter 29:

THE APPLE DOESN'T FALL FAR

I think the worst part of doing something embarrassing, is that one is hardly ever alone when it happens.

In Grandma's case, she was, quite literally, in the middle of 50,000 people. She and Grandpa were doing a show with the Sons of the Pioneers one time in the Houston Astrodome. Grandma was singing a perky little song, stepping coquettishly across the arena, when the Pioneers, who were standing behind her, noticed that her slip was slowly sliding down from under her skirt. They could hardly keep straight faces as it painfully inched its way down, finally dropping in a wad around her ankles. Without missing a beat, she glanced down, stepped right out of it, and kept singing. Both Grandpa and The Pioneers lost it at that moment, as well as everyone else in the stands.

Well, Grandma must have passed that part of her DNA down to me. She used to tell me all the time that I was "just like her." So it is with reluctance that I say, I am not a novice to embarrassing situations.

I have forgotten my music in the bathroom backstage, forcing me to improvise my viola part during an entire string quartet concerto.

I have gone right, when all the other dancers onstage are going left.

I have raised a pop tart to my ear to answer a phone call.

I applied a glue stick to my lips while driving thinking it was ChapStick.

I have missed my mouth and stuck the straw up my nose on a date.

I have accidentally worn my bathing suit inside out and backwards, while strutting around a country club.

I have rolled up my program during a concert to swat a jumping spider off a man's bald head in front of me. (Missed the spider, but got his attention.)

I have rear-ended two police officers in a squad car at a stoplight in Sacramento.

I have dropped four C batteries, down into the orchestra pit, pelting the trumpet player during a show.

I have yelled at my son, to straighten up, while fielding in a Little League game. Turns out it wasn't my son, but the boy's parents were sitting right behind me, laughing hysterically. My son wasn't on the field. In fact, it wasn't even my son's team.

I have given a serious speech about Presidents Ford and Carter, in a survey class of 300 students, referring to the candidates unintentionally as Cord and Farter. Twice.

I have mistakenly worn two right shoes to the gym to work out.

I have subbed for a high school boys' basketball class, unintentionally yelling out, "Alright boys, grab your balls and let's play."

I have watched my fake ponytail fall to the pavement while riding a palomino in the nationally televised Rose Parade on New Year's Day.

And during a small theater performance on Melrose, I forgot the words to my entire song before I even began. I stood there smiling and chatting with the audience, while my drummer and former Mouseketeer, Cubby O'Brien, sat there repeating the intro, with Stanley Livingston, from *My Three Sons* on the soundboard in back, wondering what I was doing. Oh, did I also mention that Shirley Jones and her husband, Marty, were sitting in the front row center of this small, intimate theater? Horrifying. So I told a few stories, ended with "Happy Trails", and walked proudly off the stage. Thank you! Thank you very much!

As you can see, I am familiar with awkwardness.

A few years ago, I was at the Lone Pine Film Festival, which we go to every October. On the last day of the event, there is always a parade down Main Street. Well, this particular year, Robert Wagner was one of our special guests, whom I found quite charming throughout the weekend. He said, "Please. Call me RJ." (Um, that's a little awkward, but ok.) In the final parade, RJ was a few cars ahead of the one I was in. My Aunt Cheryl, my Aunt Mimi, and I were sitting side by side on top of the convertible. I was wearing Grandpa's rhinestone, fringed Nudie shirt, which zipped up the side. It was a very warm day, and the shirt, being made of wool, was very itchy and hot. In fact, I don't know how Grandpa ever performed in it, under sweltering stage lights, without passing out.

My aunts and I were having a delightful ride, talking, laughing, and waving to the crowd. About halfway through the parade route, I thought to myself, *well at least a little breeze seems to have come up. It's really cooling off!* We got to the end of the route and RJ has just gotten out of his convertible as we rode up next to him. He immediately looked away, trying to stifle a smile. As I got out of the car, I glanced down, and there, to my horror, I saw that my entire shirt was completely unzipped all the way from my waist up to my armpit. No wonder I had felt a breeze halfway down the parade route. I had been flashing the whole town of Lone Pine along the way. I clutched my shirt and struggled with the zipper, which was now stuck. Of course, it was. As my Aunt Mimi fumbled to close my zipper, we couldn't stop laughing. We began walking back to the hotel, arguing like a couple of fishwives, about who should have noticed it first. It doesn't matter. The crowd that day, got a parade ... and a show.

Life is embarrassing. I learned two things from my grandma. First, don't take yourself so seriously, and second, always have a sense of humor. Wise words. It certainly makes me feel better to laugh with everyone at the silly predicaments I sometimes get myself into.

So, I want to assure you, that if I haven't yet done anything embarrassing in front of you, please be patient. I will get to you shortly. It's just a matter of time.

It is truly a privilege to be the custodian of the same rhinestone fringed Nudie shirt Grandpa used to wear. However, if I do venture out in it at western festivals, I now make sure that devious little side zipper stays closed with a safety pin. **Below:** Me with Robert Wagner

Chapter 30:

THE LIVES THEY TOUCHED

If you've ever wondered if Roy and Dale were genuinely that nice in person, the answer is unequivocally yes. Well, that is, except for the New York City hair incident. Two ladies were walking behind him and Grandma down the sidewalk. One of the women, not realizing who was in front of them, was clucking about her "inside knowledge" that Roy Rogers was actually bald, and wore a hairpiece. He overheard them, as they went on and on about it. Knowing that it wasn't true, he couldn't stand it anymore. He stopped and spun around, startling them both. Looking the two ladies straight in the face, he grabbed his hair and vigorously pulled it, exclaiming, "Pull it! Go ahead! You'll see it's real!" Grandma, thinking it was hilarious, howled with laughter, as the two ladies scurried away in shock and embarrassment. But other than that little incident, Grandma and Grandpa were approachable and kind to everyone, regardless of any differences. Neither of them were impressed by the Hollywood crowd. Grandpa sometimes went hunting or golfing with Clark Gable, but not for the purpose of getting good press, they just both had similar interests.

It is intriguing to me, the number of people in the movie business I have spoken to, who have credited Grandpa for either their first experience in acting or for being, in some way, a major influence in their career. Many have just gone out of their way to let me know how much they loved and respected Roy and Dale.

* * * * *

In 1998, right after Grandpa passed, I listened as Burt Reynolds talked about his own dad, who never really viewed him as a successful actor until Burt went hunting one time with Grandpa. When he went over to tell his dad about it later, his dad got real quiet for a moment. Then he spoke, "You went huntin' with Roy Rogers, huh? Ok, NOW you've made it, son!"

* * * * *

Back in 2008, a year before David Carradine's tragic death, I spent an afternoon sitting at a table with him and his wife, Annie, and son, Max. We had both been asked to be at a Celebrity Autograph Show at CBS Studios on Radford, which had been the old Republic Studio Lot years ago. Our table was set up on the outdoor New York street that was more currently familiar to me as the set used in the *Seinfeld* television sitcom.

When fans approached the table with photos for him to sign, David spoke respectfully, but very quietly, in almost a monotone voice to each person. As I carried on a bit of conversation with him in between signings, we got on the subject of his early years at Republic when his dad, John Carradine, worked there. Suddenly, there was this light in his eyes, and a softer tone in his voice, as he smiled ever so slightly. He told me of watching his dad, and my Grandpa Roy doing a scene together when he was just a young boy, peeking up curiously to watch from the nearby wash on the lot. At that moment, watching Roy, he told me that he knew, "That's what I want to do!" He sat there, suspended in his thoughts for a moment, until another fan came up, requesting an autograph. Then the dark curtain slowly went down again. Since then, my husband, Gino, and I have gotten to be good friends with his half-brother, Bobby (Robert Carradine), but it's odd to think that, in some small way, our two families were connected long before our friendship.

* * * * *

Another dear friend of mine, Rachel Greenbush, and I were also linked together through our families, years before the two of us knew each other. Her father, actor Billy Greenbush, was in Grandpa's last movie, *Macintosh and TJ.* He played the villain who punches Grandpa's character in the face. Billy was very sentimental when he found out who my grandfather was, and said, "I'm impressed by the fact that Roy would always take the time, whenever we were at the same event, to come find me and shake my hand. Your grandfather was a man of genuine honor and integrity. It wasn't just the characters he played on-screen. It was who Roy was at his core."

Now here, forty years later, his daughter Rachel and Danny, her husband, are close friends of ours. I love it when two worlds collide like this. Incidentally, Rachel and her lovely twin sister, Robyn, played the role of Carrie, the littlest Ingalls daughter on the long-running TV show, *Little House on the Prairie.* And yes, it is Carrie, who takes a face-plant in the grass while running down the hill in the beginning show credits. The sister who fell was then reluctant to keep running or do a second take, so the final cut is a composite of both girls sharing the infamous digger run. I'll leave it to you to figure out which twin was the one who actually tumbled.

* * * * *

In 2003, I was at a party in the Hollywood Hills at Countess Yola's, "Belvedere Estate," which is a landmark as well as the former home of Rudolph Valentino. While sitting outside enjoying hors d'oeuvres on her patio, Harry Morgan (Colonel Potter from the television series, *M*A*S*H**), walked over and asked if the chair next to me was free. "Sure! Have a seat," I said, as I pulled out the chair for him. We got to talking, and this seasoned actor shared with me that the first movie he ever made was with my grandpa, which had been an experience he would never forget. He was so cute, recounting every scene to me in full detail.

* * * * *

201

On another occasion at the Beverly Garland Hotel, I was talking with Stan Livingston, (actor on the 1960-1972 television series, *My Three Sons*). As we talked, he shared that he also had his first acting experience, alongside Grandpa Roy in a toy commercial.

✳ ✳ ✳ ✳ ✳

I used to watch *Leave it to Beaver* on TV. In one episode, Beaver and his best friend, Larry Mondello, were sitting on the back steps eating baloney. After they finish eating their snack, Beaver suggested to Larry that they go play "Roy Rogers and Dale Evans," making sure, of course, to let Larry know that he wanted to play Roy, leaving Larry to be Dale. I was in kindergarten at the time, and as I watched that episode with rapt attention, I was 100% certain, upon hearing Grandma and Grandpa's names come out of his mouth, that Beaver and I just had to be related. "Yes," I thought. "He's probably my cousin. I have so many of those." Two years ago, I ran into Jerry and Teresa Mathers in Burbank. Lovely couple. I shared my early scientific findings with them, but the harsh truth of the matter is that we are not related after all. Wow. Such a bitter pill to swallow. The only silver lining to that one is that I, at least, have two new friends!

✳ ✳ ✳ ✳ ✳

The Golden Boot Awards was a dinner/awards show in Beverly Hills, which veteran movie sidekick, Pat Buttram created as a way to recognize the achievements of actors, actresses, stunt people, and others who had significant involvement with film and TV Westerns. It was held in August every year, usually at The Beverly Hilton Hotel, and it ran for 25 years. Our family, being one of the original families in the start-up of the Golden Boot, was very involved, so my Aunt Cheryl would put me in charge of various jobs throughout the evening to help make the event run smoothly. I was assigned to greet different celebrities when their limos drove up to the curb, then accompany them down the red carpet, guiding them to specific interviews on the way to the green room. Throughout those years, I met many interesting people in the entertainment industry who knew my grandparents personally and had wonderful stories to tell me. One year I was to greet Fess Parker, and as we started down the red carpet, the paparazzi got the mistaken idea that we were together as a couple. "Fess, Fess! Over here! May we get a picture of you and your lovely date?"

"Uh oh," I said, as I began to set them straight.

Fess leaned over to me, and said quietly, "Awww, don't worry about it. Why don't we just give'em a little rumor to talk about for a minute!" he laughed, as he put his arm around me and posed. After we stood there smiling for a minute, and I was sufficiently blinded by the flurry of flashes, he told them who I was, and how much he revered my grandparents, which began a new conversation altogether. That year, my picture ended up in *Cowboys and Indians* magazine, and I smile to think what a kind gentleman Fess was. But I do laugh whenever I come across that picture, at how I seem to end up in the most unlikely places. By the way, they did print the correct information under my photo. I was not his date.

One year, I was in with Clint Eastwood and Morgan Freeman. In a different year, it was Tom Selleck, Sam Elliott, then James Caan, and Stefanie Powers. The year I was assigned to Lee Majors, I almost missed him, because I didn't recognize him and his new wife. On the way, he told me what an honor it was to have Grandpa guest star on his television series, *The Fall Guy*. I do remember when that show was trying to make a deal with Grandpa, who was then 71. Grandpa was nervous about remembering lines, getting back on a horse, and looking fit, so he kept turning the producers down. But Lee was so adamant about having him guest star, that the show kept sweetening the deal. Finally, it got so embarrassing that Grandpa reluctantly said yes. It was a great episode, also starring my Uncle Dusty, and ending with Peter Breck, Jim Drury, Jocko Mahoney, and John Russell, all coming to aid Roy in a grand fistfight brawl with the jewel thieves in the final scene.

Whenever I was escorting someone on the red carpet, we seemed to have more in common than you would think, which leads me back to my original conclusion. These are regular people with interesting jobs. The most revealing experience happened to me when I was in a conversation with the two Roberts (Conrad and Stack). I backed up and quickly realized I had stepped on someone's toe behind me. I turned quickly to put my hand on the person's arm and apologize when I realized it was Donald O'Connor. The first thing out of my mouth was, "Ohhhhh I love you! I ... I ... mean, in *Singin' in the Rain.*" He laughed and was very gracious, but I was mortified. Coming from a family where I had seen people gush over my grandparents time and time again, I was quite confident I would never do that myself. But there I was, face to face with Donald O'Connor and I sounded, I'm sure, like a complete idiot. I was shocked at myself. I felt similar feelings when sitting next to Dick Van Dyke at the Sinatra Golf Tournament Dinner. He was such a nice man, and we had a pleasant conversation. But I really worked at keeping it together because, in my mind, I kept lapsing into "It's a Jolly Holiday with Mary." I suppose I feel out of my comfort zone if the person isn't wearing cowboy boots, with a six-shooter on their hip. Who knows?

* * * * *

I do have fond memories of Mickey Rooney at the 22nd Golden Boot Awards inside the Sheraton Universal Hotel. I got him and his wife seated right away, per their request, before anyone else in the ballroom had arrived, and asked if I could get anything for them. He said, "Why don't you sit down with us for a few minutes and chat?" So we sat there in the cool, quiet ballroom with no one else around and just talked about this and that. He too had a wealth of memories and very kind things to say about Grandma and Grandpa.

* * * * *

I was sharing a story the other day with Dawn Moore, the daughter of Clayton Moore, more commonly known as The Lone Ranger from the 1950s TV Western series. We realized that sometimes, people have confused my grandpa with her dad. I've had people say to me, "Oh yes, your grandpa was the cowboy with the mask." Dawn shared with me that she has heard people comment, "I love your dad and his horse, Trigger."

"Well," I said, "at least no one has ever asked either of us if we can get them tickets to an Angels game." (For some who may not remember, Gene Autry was the original owner of the Anaheim Angels.)

Surprisingly, I spoke with Hugh Hefner several times. Each time we talked, he spoke very highly of Grandma and Grandpa, and it was apparent, even though his lifestyle was obviously very different from Roy and Dale, he still had the utmost respect for them, telling me that they were "not only icons in the Western genre, but were role models for a generation of kids." Hef was a big film buff, donating thousands of dollars to the film department at UCLA to help restore old movies, or "pictures," as the older generations used to call them.

Diamond Farnsworth, who is the second unit director and stunt double for Mark Harmon, on the TV series, NCIS, also had a father who was one of Grandpa's stuntmen, Richard Farnsworth. Our families go way back together. Most importantly, however, Diamond and his amazing wife, Linda, are two of our best friends. Having lived just ten minutes from each other, we have had a standing breakfast appointment every weekend together for many years.

My older friend and mentor, Peggy Stewart, was also a leading lady in the B-Westerns at Republic Studios during the same time as my grandparents. She and Grandma were good friends. The television series she was on, called *Red Ryder*, was filmed on the same lot as *The Roy Rogers Show*, and she would reminisce about how she preferred to spend her breaks over on Roy and Dale's set because it was a lot more fun and they treated the crew like family. Peggy passed away at 94 years old in 2019. My life is better because of those years with her presence in it.

* * * * *

I guess the reason I feel compelled to share all of these snippets of conversations, is because these people were their peers, and it is odd but wonderful to hear stories from those that I wouldn't even be talking to, had it not been solely because of my grandparents.

I'm a kindergarten teacher. I spend my days teaching 5-year-olds how to read, and saying things I never thought I'd hear myself say like, "Please stop licking my knee," and "take the scissors out of your underwear, and pull up your pants." So there is really no threat of me believing I am someone on the "Who's Who" list. Roy and Dale touched the lives of a variety, even a strange mixture, of individuals, that's for sure. They could relate to anyone, young or old, prominent or obscure, rich or poor.

The takeaway for me is gratefulness. I was privileged to know these two people I called Grandma and Grandpa outside of their spotlight. I could live in my world of normality most of the time. But then, at a moment's notice, they would reach for my hand and gently pull me into a different world for short periods of time to experience pretty fantastic things, without all of the responsibility that comes with fame. Because of them, I now have people in my life that are precious to me, none of which happened on my account. In essence, it's because I lived on the edge of their spotlight.

Longtime friends, Diamond and Linda Farnsworth

My dear friend friend, Peggy Stewart who worked with my grandparents at Republic Studios in the B-Westerns during the 1940s. She continued working almost until the time of her death in 2019, picking up guest roles on *Seinfeld*, *Frasier*, *The Office*, and even a movie with Adam Sandler.

Charlotte Stewart (who played the role of Miss Beadle – *Little House on the Prairie*) told me she had her heart broken when she raced home from a skating party to see Roy Rogers, who was meeting her dad at their home for business. There he was in her front yard as she drove up. She flung the car door open, but forgot she still had her roller skates on. She fell and did a face plant right in front of Roy. Mortified, and all scraped up, she ran to her room and never got to meet her hero.

With Clint Eastwood at the Golden Boot Awards 2006.

I've heard Burt Reynolds say that his dad never considered him a big star until he went hunting one day with Roy Rogers. "NOW you're a star son!"

Every time Bobby Carradine comes over, he gently sifts through to find only the black jelly beans, so I bought him his own little glass jar, with only black jelly beans. It's become a routine.

Spent a day signing pictures with David Carradine and his wife, Annie at CBS Studios.

Lee Majors wanted Grandpa on his show, *The Fall Guy*, but he had to do a little arm twisting to make it happen.

Having fun with Harry Morgan.

After dinner at The Sportsman's Lodge with the Sons of the Pioneers.

At the table for dinner with Dick Van Dyke, Palm Springs 2005.

Chapter 31:

TOM FOX, DALE'S SON

You know, my dad, Tom, was the oldest of the Rogers nine children. Not much has been written about him, and public photos of my dad have been few. I would be remiss if I didn't share a bit about Tom Fox, because his story was most definitely meant to be, and had a profound impact on the personal and public lives of Roy and Dale.

Tom's story begins with his mom, who wasn't always "Dale Evans." She was born, "Frances Octavia Smith." She was a precocious child, spending as much time as she could, pirouetting in front of a mirror, pretending to be an actress. She would tell me that she loved to sing and would perform for anyone at the drop of a hat. Then when she was three years old, her little brother, Hillman Jr. was born, and they called him, "Son." She adored Son, but she wanted nothing more than to grow up. So at fourteen years old, she left her family and eloped with her eighteen-year-old boyfriend, Thomas Fox, over the border to Arkansas, which crushed her parents.

After marrying, and becoming now, "Frances Fox," they headed on to Tennessee, where she soon discovered she was pregnant. When she was fifteen, she gave birth to my dad, Thomas Fox Jr., in Memphis, on November 28, 1927. Soon after, her husband left her and little Tommy, claiming he was too young to be burdened with the responsibility of a wife and son. She couldn't face the fact that she was now a single mom, and couldn't bring herself to file the divorce papers until she was seventeen. By then, she was already a struggling, single mom. But when her mother, Betty Sue Smith, offered to adopt little Tommy, Frances was too proud and stubborn to agree to that. Her mom, Betty Sue, however, did care for him while she went back to school to become a stenographer. When Tommy began to talk, he called his Grandma Smith, "Mom," and he called his real mother, "Sassy," because he couldn't pronounce "Frances." Even though they never kept it a secret from him that his real mother was actually Frances, I am not sure how he was able to process all of this as a young boy.

In the years that followed, Frances changed her name to "Dale," and vigorously pursued fame. While trying to balance her day job as a stenographer, and slowly breaking into radio by singing in the evenings, her schedule left little time for raising a son. The radio station also decided she needed a more contemporary name for a singer, the kind that rolls off the tongue easily over the radio. So from then on, she became Dale Evans. They moved from Arkansas to Memphis, then Chicago, Kentucky, Texas, and back to Chicago. After two failed marriages, one to August "Candy" Johns, and the next to Dale Butts, she so desperately wanted stability for her son, but she would not give up her insatiable quest for fame at any cost. She and Tommy were living in Chicago, existing on a shared can of beans a day, when she hit rock bottom. She became severely anemic, and Tommy developed a raging ear infection, spiking a high fever. When taken to urgent care, they found that he also had a bad case of rickets, from malnutrition. She had reached a breaking point. She knew that the life she was living was not conducive to raising a small child. Tommy needed a safer and healthier place to live, so she finally relented to her mom's offer, sending Tommy to live on the farm with his grandparents from the age of nine until almost thirteen. He flourished there. It was probably the best thing that ever happened to him. Life became stable, his physical health improved, he had friends his own age, and the farm was his playground. He was taught family values while attending Boy Scouts and Sunday School.

Dale's life was a study in contradictions at this point. In those days, women stayed home with their children, and she wanted so much to be successful as a single mom, in providing that sort of stable home life for Tommy. But on the other hand, she was a fiercely independent, strong-willed woman with a voracious drive to get out in the public eye to become famous, which caused constant tension. She was, in a sense, an early feminist before there was even a name for that.

But Dale still struggled with the pangs of guilt. Four years later, Dale missed her son, and sent for him, now thirteen, to come live with her again in Chicago. She had hopes of successfully reuniting with her son while continuing to pursue fame. When she got her first big break to go to Hollywood, she was working at the elite Chez Paree nightclub, in Chicago, alongside Jimmy Durante and Ray Bolger, who had just finished his screen portrayal of the Scarecrow in *The Wizard of Oz*. She had been discouraged that her reviews were less than she had hoped for, so Ray Bolger stopped by her dressing room after the show one night, and encouraged her to freshen up her part in the show by doing an original song, something that would make her stand out from all the others. She came up with a little song called, "Will You Marry Me, Mr. Laramie?" He liked it and offered to "stooge" for her onstage while she sang. It became an instant success.

A CBS executive, who was in the audience that night, liked her, and she was offered a contract with a radio affiliate there in Chicago. One thing led to another, and the radio program reached Los Angeles, where a talent scout heard her, saw her photos, and thought she might be the new fresh face they needed for a movie musical called, Holiday Inn, with Fred Astaire and Bing Crosby. It meant she would need to fly to Los Angeles.

Dale went home and talked to Tommy, who was now fourteen and preferred to be called Tom. He was supportive of her exploring this new opportunity if this was what she felt she needed to do. So she flew to Los Angeles, in 1941, to meet with the head of talent and casting at Paramount Pictures Studio. With the intent to screen test for the Christmas movie, she bent under the pressure of the talent scout. She fibbed about her age, her dancing ability (or lack thereof), and had been told to conceal the fact that she had a teenage son, or she would be considered, "not as marketable" in Hollywood. She was to tell everyone that her son, Tom, was her younger brother.

Tom, after having been shuffled around between step-dads, neighbors, babysitters, and other family members, during his unsettling childhood, was now facing another hurdle, to stay in the shadows, so she could further her career. However, after living on the farm in Texas with Grandma Smith, he had now become a solid young man of principles, who had given his life to God, and he felt uncomfortable pretending he was her brother. "I understand. You do what you have to do, Mom," he said. "I won't tell anyone that I am your son, but I won't lie about it either, so I will just make myself scarce." He stayed away from the public eye, avoiding the press for four years. Tom did work part-time, however, in the fan mail office, opening and sorting their fan mail for them. In 1945, he enrolled at USC, still hiding the fact of being Dale's son.

Tom's identity finally came out publicly in 1946 when, at nineteen, he enlisted in the Army, and was required to give the name of his parent. Someone then leaked it to the paper, and Dale was freed from this ongoing lie. Roy and Tom had a solid relationship, and Tom began calling Dale "Mom," and Roy "Dad," around the time of their wedding.

Dale took on a new role of being a stepmother to Roy's three small children, Cheryl, Linda Lou, and Dusty. The two older girls, seven and four, resented Dale, thinking she sought to take their mom's place. Roy was working long hours and Dale felt overwhelmed. She confided in Tom one day, and as they talked, he suggested that maybe she might want to take a moment to get grounded and go to church with him the next day. So she did. As Grandma would tell me later, the sermon was about building your house upon the Rock, and that a home built on faith in God will withstand any storms that may come. She was sure the pastor was pointing his words directly at her. At the end of the service, Tom saw the conflict in her eyes. He quietly asked her if she was open to letting God help her find the peace that she had been looking for, for so long. She hesitated. Seeing the sadness on his face, she went home that night, feeling completely broken. She laid her life before God, and she said the next Sunday, she nearly flew out of her seat at the end of the sermon to pray with one of the pastors. She vowed she would never pressure Grandpa into making that kind of decision, and she didn't. But she had changed, in a dramatically positive way. Not long after, Grandpa also made the decision to follow Christ, and from that point on, their parenting, their personal lives, as well as their public persona gained a new dimension. Their faith was driving them now, instead of their egos. So, it would have been impossible to write a book without including their transformation. Even though they never forced their faith on others, trusting God became the focal point of their life and breath for the rest of their lives. And it all began, simply with a young son praying for his mom, and God listened.

Grandma told me in her last years, that she had struggled with tremendous guilt over the way she raised my dad. This may have been the reason why she sometimes seemed to spend a little more time with us, almost as if she was trying to make up for the years she missed with him. My dad could have been bitter or resentful. But he wasn't. He loved unconditionally. I asked him one time, how he was able to stay so positive, even in the hardest of situations. He answered, "Well, you can either focus on the negative things, or the positive things in life, and whichever one you choose, gets easier to do." My dad wasn't full of empty words. He authentically lived that. He was forgiving, kind, and genuinely the happiest person I have ever known. Growing up, I could often see how much Grandma adored Dad, and how much Grandpa respected him. What could have been a disastrous outcome, between mother and son, was beautifully woven into a tapestry no one would have expected, which had a ripple effect throughout the entire family. I don't know exactly how or why life happens the way it does, but I do know that Tom Fox's story was definitely meant to be.

Thomas Frederick Fox 1927-2012

Dale as a toddler.

Dale with her parents. They used to say, "Frances was always headstrong."

Leaving home, seeking stardom.

As a rising star, Dale had little time for raising a son.

Tom (left) in middle school with a friend.

Tom in high school looking as though he's posing for a Fritos commercial.

My mom, Barb, and Dale with Tom getting the wedding license.

Aunt Cheryl and Aunt Linda Lou were junior
bridesmaids in my parents' wedding.

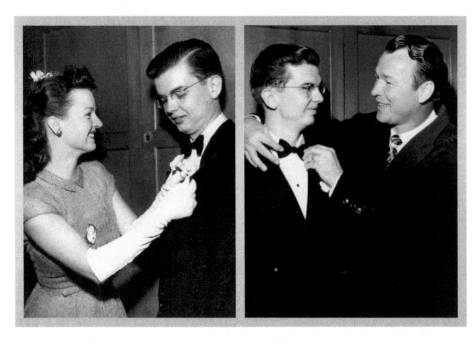

Dale, Roy and Tom putting on the final touches.

The groom's parents watch as Tom and Barbara cut the cake.

Chapter 32:

HE WAS ALSO MY DAD

Tom Fox was indeed Dale Evans' only biological son, but more importantly, he was also my dad. He was an insanely talented musician. The flute was his primary instrument. He also played piano, string bass, bells, drums, and pretty much every woodwind and brass instrument in the band. He arranged music, sang solos, and directed choirs and orchestras. But in the most loving way, I have to say, that he was every bit "classic nerd" at its finest. Most of his life, he wore a crew cut, told embarrassing "dad jokes," and paired his summer shorts, with dark socks and dress shoes. He rocked the pen protector in his pocket, completing the look with the clip-on sunglasses over his other ones. Finally, on summer vacations, he had his camera slung around his neck on one side, and his binoculars on the other, even at times, adding a tape recorder hanging in front, to catch moments of family mirth along the journey. The only real snag in that was that he rarely caught any spontaneous audio, so he would ask us to repeat it, which resulted in a lot of, "Da-a-a-ad!" recordings. To round everything off, you could always see his two-inch-thick wallet bulging from his back pocket.

However, my dad also had the sweetest nature. Over the course of my lifetime, I can count on one hand how many times I saw him upset, though there were certainly many times he could have been. He had the patience of Job, raising three daughters who were always running late, for he was never late. He had missed a train when he was ten, and he never forgot the feeling of seeing it pulling away from the station without him. As a result, he was passionate about punctuality. "Alright girls, we're leaving in 15 minutes! ... 10 minutes ... 5 minutes ... I'm starting the engine!" He would count down, as we scrambled into the car, our arms full of socks and shoes, make-up, and hairbrushes.

In my teenage years, it used to irritate me when he asked so many questions when I came home from an event. It wasn't until I realized he wasn't prying, but that he was just plain interested, that I began to find it endearing. He had an innocence about him, which held no ulterior motives. When other people in my family would sometimes find my whirlwind of a personality irritating, he would sit back and relish it with a big smile. He would sometimes even laugh when I burst through the front door with some drama. I would then stop, and with a sense of irritation ask, "What's so funny?!" He would affectionately say, "I don't know. I just really enjoy you, that's all." I always knew that he not only loved me, but he truly liked me. He embraced my quirks and flaws unconditionally. I felt cherished by him. He would listen to my feelings without judgment, much like what I had in my relationship with Grandma Dale, as well. The two of them were in many ways, alike.

He had a true teacher's heart. When we took the train to Texas one summer to visit family, he studied up on all of the flora and fauna we would see out the windows along the way. Then he would sit at dinner with us, and wiggle the kitchen table while we ate, to give us an idea of how it would feel to eat meals on a moving train. My parents were both teachers. We had two months off as a family, so we visited a different part of the United States in our camping trailer every summer until we had seen all but two of the fifty states. When driving through Arizona and Utah, my parents would stop alongside the road to help us collect a bit of red dirt. Then at our next stop, we would find a picnic table and mix the dirt with water, fashioning small pots and bowls with it. Then we would bake our creations in the trailer oven, while we learned about the tribes of that area. They both would help us collect pamphlets, postcards, and stickers from each place we stopped on our road trips so that we could make a summer scrapbook of our vacation each year.

My dad encouraged curiosity and discovery by bringing various instruments home for us to try for fun on the weekends from his band room at Rosemont Junior High. One Sunday afternoon, in particular, I remember crawling up inside a big, shiny sousaphone that he had set up on our front lawn. "Go ahead, honey! Let's see if we can get a sound out of this thing!" So I took the biggest breath ever, cupped my hands around the mouthpiece, and gave it my best blow like there was no tomorrow. It tickled my lips, and somewhere deep within that cavernous horn, I heard a robust rumble blurt out. My dad laughed with delight, and I remember feeling pleased with myself. I knew I could do whatever my dad asked of me, because I trusted, knowing he wouldn't ever ask me something I wasn't capable of. He challenged me like that for the rest of my life, and I ended up far exceeding what I ever imagined possible.

I feel blessed for having had Tom Fox as my dad. His love was constant and I never doubted that. Thankfully, he never lectured or told me how to live. He didn't have to. He just showed me by his example.

Dad helping me with my homework.

I distinctly remember crawling up inside the sousaphone that day in my blue Sunday dress, and kneeling on the square green stool. Quite possibly the biggest breath I'd ever taken at 4-years-old.

Tom Fox playing his flute for a wedding reception.

My dad and mom, Tom and Barbara Fox, by the front gate of
Grandma and Grandpa's house in Apple Valley, CA.

My dad and me in 2011, a year before he passed. He was in and out of the hospital a lot with congestive heart failure, and I would always tease him about the way he sincerely raved about the hospital food. "You're just weird, Dad. No one likes hospital food." He was truly the most positive person I have ever known. We had a very special relationship.

Dad, my son Trevor, and Grandma. Lunch at Scoma's on the Wharf in San Francisco. She loved visiting "The City" more than anywhere else.

Even as they grew older, they would still get confused for brother and sister.

Chapter 33:

OUT OF MY COMFORT ZONE

My grandparents were quite synonymous with the term B-Westerns. You cannot utter the names "Roy and Dale" without conjuring up images of horses, white hats, and maybe a finely tuned guitar. Grandma and Grandpa packed just about as much as anyone could have into the years they were given. And while B-Westerns have long since gone by the wayside, the honesty, respect, and integrity Roy and Dale brought to the world back then are still relevant today. They were far from perfect and would be the first ones to admit that. But God, in His grace, touched many people through them because they were willing to step out of their comfort zone.

Toward the end of my grandparents' lives, it became quite apparent that a few of us in this big melting pot we call, "The Rogers Family," might want to step up in order to keep Roy and Dale's legacy alive. I didn't go looking for it, but when the "Wheel of Responsibility" was spun, it somehow landed on my name. Well, I didn't win a car or a trip to Tahiti, but I have collected priceless experiences. For the last twenty years, I have been out and about and across the country, to western festivals, fairs, and rodeos to sing, tell stories, sit on panels, ride in parades, and spend time one-on-one with fans of my grandparents to give them a glimpse of what it was like growing up with Roy and Dale back in the day. I am not a "star," Western or otherwise. However, I am one small link to a unique couple that endeared themselves to millions. I am honored to do it for as long as people are still asking for it. When I travel, most of the responsibilities are well within my scope. But occasionally, I have come upon some unexpected situations that are out of my comfort zone.

Dean and Debbie Smith are wonderful friends, and Dean was the last stunt man to double Grandpa in his final movie, *Macintosh and TJ,* in 1975. They invited me to come to perform at the "Dean Smith Celebrity Rodeo" in Abilene, Texas, back in 2006. When I arrived, I was told that in addition to singing in the program that evening, I would also be participating in one of the opening night's rodeo events, "Team Penning." Two things here ... first of all, I didn't even know what Team Penning was, much less how to do it. And second of all, I was told that I would be competing against the actor Wilford Brimley and his team. Not Wilford. Seriously? "He never smiles," I whispered under my breath. I couldn't stop my mind from racing. I can herd 5-year-olds across a playground, but cows across an arena are a completely different kind of polka.

After rifling frantically through my phone for information, I found that basically, Team Penning is a timed event that involves three riders and their horses riding as a team, to move three specific cows out of the herd and into a pen on the other side of the arena in 60 seconds. Well, the first problem for me was the "60 seconds" part. Umm, right. I'll still be getting my foot in the stirrup while the other team is doing a victory lap with their cows. But after that, there was an even bigger problem. This so-called "pen" they were referring to was yawning wide open at BOTH ends. *It's going to be like threading beads on a string with no knot on the end,* I thought to myself.

The team leader sensed my hesitancy and gave me the easiest job. He said, "Ride over and guard the far opening so when we get each cow in the pen, they don't run out the other side." Hmm. Sounds easy enough. Ok, I got it. The buzzer rang, and out we galloped as the announcer called out the number 5. There were 30 cows in the arena, three of which, were marked with the number 5. I scanned the herd while making a beeline for my post. My horse and I stood at the opening, but I noticed that there was also an alleyway between the pen and the wall, where the cows could sneak down the side and get away. Now I was so nervous; I was shaking like a beetle on a pin. I was clearly out of my comfort zone. The crowd was cheering and shouting, and the cows were agitated, bumping and side-swiping me this way and that. Seriously, at that point, I was thinking, if a clown invited me into the woods right now, I would just go.

Suddenly, one of my teammates shouted at me to stand guard as he herded one of them into the pen. Then he flipped around to go get another cow. Ok, here we go. Game on! I said to myself. Unfortunately for me, this penned cow trotted right out of the other end and started down the side toward me to make her get-away. As she did, I rode over to block her. I guess my inner educator kicked in, and before I could stop myself, I pointed my finger at the cow, and called out sternly to her in my best "teacher" voice, "NOOO!" The cow looked up, and I noticed the whites of her eyes as she stopped. The nice cowboys along the railing beside me doubled over with laughter. "Ohhh! So THAT'S how it's done!" they guffawed. I responded, "YES ... YES, IT IS! That's EXACTLY how it's done!" I couldn't help laughing along with them. Although I was somewhat embarrassed, I felt pleased that my unintentional technique had actually worked. Well, we didn't win, but I didn't embarrass my team, either. However, the story of my little escapade got some good mileage all weekend long, and to this day, people still ask me about it.

Afterward, I rode over to Wilford to congratulate him. "Thanks!" he said gruffly. Then he added, "Would ya take a picture of me and my best friend here?" I said, "Sure!" and greeted the man, who was also on horseback. Wilford handed me his phone. I took his picture, but when I gave it back to him, he had his thumb over the lens and accidentally snapped a second picture. When he checked the photo, all he saw was the photo he had just taken of his thumb. He mumbled, "Ya got yer thumb in the way! Ya gotta take it again!" I tried to explain what he had done, but he was impatient. So I just went ahead and took the second photo of them. I handed it back and there he went again, snapping the second picture of his thumb. At that point, I was clearly telling him that it was HIS thumb and that I did take two good photos if he would just take a minute to look. But he made me do it again, and now I was starting to laugh. He wasn't. He was actually a little irritated. After the third time, and the third picture of his thumb, he said, "Never mind." I smiled and said, "Don't worry, Wilford. You've got some good photos there." As I rode off, I muttered under my breath, "Three of you two, and three of your thumb." I really liked him. Gruff? Yes. But he was a good man underneath all of the grouchiness ... and besides, he won me fair and square at Team Penning.

Over the years, I have found that whenever I step outside of my comfort zone, delightful things usually happen. Even writing this book falls into that category, as this began simply as a journal to give to my sons. But during the process, I have taken a detour through an entirely different forest. The reminiscing has been cathartic as I've been able to relive so many childhood memories, in particular with my grandparents. Little did I know back then at 5 years old, that one day, forty years later, our positions would be reversed, allowing me to give back to them during their last days on earth. Life came full circle.

Many of the stories written in these pages, were the same ones we reminisced about at their bedside. Songs were sung, and music was played. We laughed. We cried. One evening, after the hospice nurse had left, my sisters and I were practicing a vocal trio in the living room, and when we turned around, proud Grandma and Grandpa were both sitting there in their wheelchairs, beaming, misty-eyed, and too choked up to speak. It was then that I realized the winds had shifted. After all those years of their family watching them perform, here they were now in the quietness of the living room, watching us with hearts full of love and admiration.

Grandpa passed quietly on July 6, 1998, at the age of 86. Grandma left this earth on February 7, 2001, at the age of 88. The last words I heard from both of them were, "I love you too, honey." It was a precious time, and even through my tears, I knew that I would see them again. Until that day, I will leave you with Grandma's own words that she wrote out herself for her memorial, or "graduation," as she loved to say.

Dale Evans Rogers
Queen of the West
October 31, 1912-February 7, 2001

BE HAPPY FOR ME! It was for this: to glorify my God and Saviour: that I was born. Please do not grieve for me. REJOICE! – that my pilgrimage is over and I am now HOME. Praise to almighty God the miraculous work of Jesus Christ in my life – for the way He wonderfully saved my soul in the spring of 1948 – when He gave me a new life centered in Him – a rich cup of life with every experience He deemed necessary for my growth as a Christian and a child of God.

If, at this time, the Lord would grant me one wish for you – one last wish, it would be this: that you experience and know the reality of Jesus Christ in your life. To know Him and to follow Him is to LIVE – now and for eternity. My Lord Jesus said, "I go to prepare a place for you, that where I am, ye might be also; in My Father's House are many mansions. If it were not so, I would have told you."

BE HAPPY FOR ME! I am now with my beloved Roy and until we meet again, may God abundantly bless you and keep you in the Light of His Matchless Love,

In Christ,

Dale Evans Rogers

The entire Rogers family at Grandma's memorial. She specifically asked us not wear dark colors; it was to be a celebration. I wore lime green there in the center. Just sayin'.

Aunt Dodie and I at the Roy Rogers Festival in Portsmouth, OH

With the boys in Lone Pine. **From left to right:** Rob Word, Darby Hinton, Robert Carradine, Diamond Farnsworth, and Wyatt McCrea.

Wilford Brimley and me.

Being interviewed at The Autry Museum of Western Heritage in
Burbank, CA at the "Cowboys of the Silver Screen" First Day of Issue
Stamp Ceremony, April 17, 2010

Hiking with Rachel Lindsay Greenbush (Carrie on Little House on the Prairie) and her husband, Danny Sanchez.

What can I say about Patrick Wayne? Just make sure (not if, but when,) he tells a joke or a funny story at the dinner table, that your mouth is not full of liquid, because it will end up on the person across from you.

HERE AND THERE

Above: Grandpa had a soft heart for kids ... maybe because he sort of was one himself. **Opposite page top:** Trigger signing in at the hotel front desk. **Opposite page bottom:** Trigger and Roy getting some much-needed shut eye.

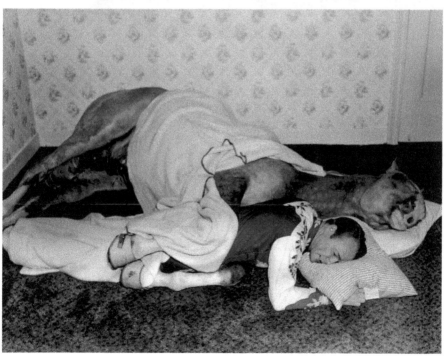

On the set of *Son of Paleface* on the Paramount lot.

Above: Frank Sinatra, Sammy Kaye, Roy, and Lou Costello discuss last minute details backstage before a performance. **Below:** Jimmy Stewart, Dale, and Roy doing a radio theater show.

Above: Moments in time with Walt Disney. **Below:** Grandpa with Ronald Reagan. My favorite part of this picture is the guy in the background. **Opposite page:** Roy with Walt Disney-- *Pecos Bill*.

Above: Roy and Dale with Don Knotts on the Andy Williams Show. **Below:** Thirty years later, I called Andy in Branson, left a message with his secretary, and 10 minutes later he called me back, reminiscing about Grandma and Grandpa. Then he left tickets for us to catch his show that evening.

Above: Roy and Babe Ruth at a children's charity fundraiser event. **Below:** Bing Crosby had Roy as a guest on his radio show.

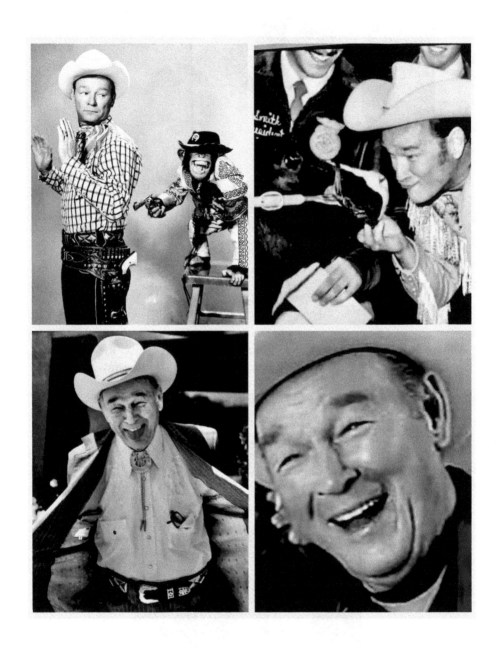

Even though Roy was seemingly shy and quiet, he had a great sense of humor. Little known fact, Grandpa Roy was the singing voice for Elmer Fudd in the 1938 short called "A Feud There Was."

ABOUT THE AUTHOR

I have had a very full life, apart from being in the Rogers family. I was born in Pasadena, California, and studied piano and viola at a very young age. I majored in Music at Biola University in Los Angeles, but quickly realized I didn't have the passion to pursue a music career. So I switched my major to Elementary Education. I did, however, continue playing viola in several quartets, and a local symphony. Then later, after moving to Germany, I was the principal violist in the Munich Chamber Orchestra, where we played concerts at the Nymphenburg Palace.

My first job ever was at Disneyland. I began on Main Street at the Coca-Cola Refreshment corner, but soon found my groove in the castle courtyard shops in Fantasyland. If you have ever been to a Disney Park and bought a pair of Mickey's ears, you'll know about the yellow stitched cursive name you can have sewn on the back of a hat. Well, one summer, we were short-staffed of people to do that. So I volunteered. I trained to be a "writer" in the Mad Hatter Shop, which, in those days, meant that you would personally sew or "write" custom names on the hats that guests had just paid for. To be trained meant we had to spend our shifts in the basement underneath Fantasyland, wearing earplugs and practicing on industrial-strength sewing machines that sounded like jackhammers. We spent hours sharpening our dexterity by sewing names with yellow thread on thick paper towels. After a week, I passed and was ready to go "on stage" with my new skill.

Upstairs in the Mad Hatter, I was nervous, and wouldn't you know, that my first guest stepped up to the counter and wanted his name, "Abdulazizahsan" sewn on a Mickey Mouse ear hat. I stared blankly at him. "Excuse me, can you say that one more time?" He repeated it. Ok now my heart is racing like a rabbit and I'm starting to sweat. "Ummm ... Do you, by any chance, have a shorter nickname?" I asked nervously. He stared at me. "No? Ok, well maybe you could write your name down for me?" I asked, as I slowly slid him a pad of paper. I tried earnestly to sew that name, but after ripping out my attempts three times, the black felt on the hat was now disintegrating. So I grabbed another hat, pleading with my shift lead under my breath, to switch places and write this one for me, just this once. "Nope," he said. Well, I got through it, but nothing about that hat was pretty, and my guest frowned as he walked away. Rough start. I eventually became one of the best writers in the shop, and people would move over into my line when they saw my finishing touches of curly ques and flowers at the end of names. Today, all of the Disney parks use automated sewing machines to custom write on all of the hats. These machines spit out perfect names, but it's not personal anymore. "Cheaters," I whisper under my breath. Such it is with progress.

I graduated with my Bachelor's Degree in Liberal Studies and my California elementary teaching credential. Along the way, I taught calligraphy, worked as a graphic artist for a print and t-shirt company in Anaheim, took quilting classes, joined a quilters group, and made stained glass.

I lived for one year with my first husband, Keric Ashley, in the African Congo, where we both taught school in a jungle village of little round straw huts, called Rwanguba. That right there is another whole book. We then moved to Europe, living in Germany for seven more years. We taught school at three American military bases consecutively and traveled around the world to 34 different countries.

When we came back to the U.S. I sang and performed for a few years around the country for western festivals, with my two sisters, in a group called The Rogers' Legacy. We also spent some wonderful times doing joint concerts with my Uncle Dusty and his band in Branson at our family museum there.

In 2002, thanks to my Aunt Cheryl, I began riding horseback in the Pasadena Rose Parade on New Year's Day. I rode in a Western group called, "The Sons and Daughters of The 'Reel' West," referring, of course, to the film cowboys. So John Wayne, Richard Farnsworth, Roy Rogers, June Lockhart, Buddy Ebsen, Joel McCrea, and funny as it sounds, Dan Rowan (comedian from the TV show "Laugh-In") were represented. We did a double take at Dan Rowan's name, asking Tom Rowan, Dan's son, how he ended up in the group. He replied that his dad had acted in one spaghetti Western. We all laughed, good-naturedly teasing him that he got in by the skin of his teeth on that one. He never did live that down. Such a good sport! I also rode three times with the Long Beach Mounted Police in the parade.

The most exciting parade year was when RFD-TV had a float with Trigger and Bullet on it, in honor of what would have been Grandpa's 100th birthday. My sons and I volunteered, spending hours gluing the petals on this float as it sat in a long line of floats in one of the float barns, and on the day of the parade, a group of 100 golden palominos just like Trigger rode in formation in front of the float, on which my aunts and uncles were riding on. It was my honor to be able to precede the float on my palomino, as it made its way for 5 and a half miles down Colorado Blvd on New Year's Day.

During those years, I taught elementary school, getting moved around somehow to every grade level from K-6. I win the award for the most flexible teacher, I guess. Yahtzee! On the weekends, I co-hosted a Saturday morning talk show on KHTS-AM radio called "Around the Barn." We interviewed actors, singers, authors, and other people in the public eye of the Western genre. "How did I get into THAT?" You say. Well, I was one of their guests, and it went so well, they just asked me to stay. So I did. I've always been one to try new things.

I was a single mom for five years, and when Keric and I remarried (other people), the four of us became good friends, spending holidays together, and we even took a summer cruise to Mexico with our three sons. Keric eventually went on to become the Deputy Superintendent of

California Schools, working with his boss, the State Superintendent, and Governor Arnold Schwarzenegger in Sacramento. He has continued to be a good friend and confidant when I've needed educational guidance.

My husband, Gino Pomilia, is a baseball coach from Marin County in Northern California, who spent some time playing for the St. Louis Cardinals farm league early on. He is Italian/Sicilian, and it took me a quick minute to realize that people in his family yell in simple conversation. He also assumes that everyone must have grown up in a home where the couches were covered in plastic, and front yards needed statues. What an interesting ride it has been. We both retired from teaching in California after thirty-three years, and we have since moved from Los Angeles to the Nevada side of Lake Tahoe. We have some property with two palominos, a pony, a miniature donkey, and four Border Collies who try to herd everyone, including the cat next door. We run the "Gino Pomilia Baseball Camp" every summer for youth, in Larkspur, CA., which has been going strong for over twenty years now.

Gino and me

Gino has a grown son named John Dominic (JD for short). JD is a firefighter, and very much like his dad in his sincere love for rural living with dogs and horses. He also played baseball at USC and visits us often.

I also have three grown sons who all remember Gigi and Grampy well. My oldest, Taylor, seems to effortlessly excel at whatever he tries. He is easygoing, which at times, makes him hilariously funny, as he strides calmly through life with a dry sense of humor. He graduated summa cum laude from his class in the school of Television, Film, and New Media at San Diego State University. After several apprenticeships on television shows, and a job with the San Diego Chargers, filming practices for the coaches to review, and assisting in the filming of their games, he opted instead for a job in videography production for a company in California called "Amari Productions" that specializes in uniquely capturing the raw and real moments at weddings.

Taylor's delightful wife, Emily, works in public relations and is always optimistic, sociable, and ready to organize a party. She is truthful, friendly, and unable to stand still when the music starts. She is perfect for Taylor. They live in California and recently made us grandparents for the first time when our little grandson, Aiden, was born last year.

A side note to the following "hat" pictures with Grampy. He used to ask for and look forward to doing the "hat" picture, as he called it, with the great-grandchildren. He'd sit them on his lap and play with them with one of his hats.

Taylor wearing Grampy's hat.   Taylor, Emily and Aiden.

My middle son, Trevor, is a wild card ... a glow fish in a tide pool of limpets. You never have to wonder what he is thinking. He'll tell you. He is creative, entrepreneurial, and unashamedly loves Denny's. When his brothers played a classical piece on the piano for the school talent show, he organized an act called, "Disco Clowns on Scooters," which was just as weird as it sounds. He teaches 6th grade and always has a quirky approach to life. His adorable wife, Arianna, is also an elementary school teacher and an avid reader. She is genuine, kind, and quiet but not shy. Arianna loves pasta, so Gino has claimed her as part Italian. She is the perfect match for Trevor.

Trevor wearing Grampy's hat.

Trevor and Arianna

My youngest son, Brendan, was born smiling. In fact, when he was a toddler, his uncle dubbed him, "The Little Happy Heart." As a toddler, he could frequently be heard saying, with authentic vigor, "It's a GOOD DAY! And 'Lasterday' was also a GOOD DAY!" We're still not sure when "lasterday" was, but he has carried that positive disposition into adulthood, always game for just about anything. He is now a middle school English teacher; and has come a long way from forgetting to wear shoes to soccer practice. His sweet wife, Abbi, is about the size of a bag of peanuts. She is a nurse and quick to help others. Abbi is perfect for Brendan. They also had our first little granddaughter, Madelyn, with a little boy now on the way, named Benjamin Thomas. "Thomas" after my dad.

Brendan wearing Grampy's hat.   Brendan, Abbi, and Madelyn

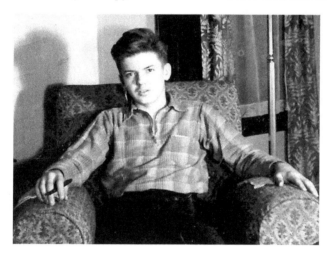

My dad, Tom Fox **(above)** was "Papa" to my sons. He made an indelible imprint on their lives. For my boys to see these rare photos of him for the first time will make "lasterday" a good day.

This book was originally a gift for them and still is. They were my sole purpose for writing these stories, and it was to be a Christmas present, a keepsake. I wanted them to get a glimpse into my childhood and a written account of some of their family history. I have to admit that I was also cathartically writing it for myself as well, because, in these uncertain times, it feels good to go back to simpler days, recalling the magical and very positive upbringing I experienced.

Then somewhere along the way, several people encouraged me to widen my audience as maybe others might want to hear these same stories, so here we are. You picked up this book for one or more of a variety of reasons. Maybe Roy and Dale are nostalgic for you, maybe your parents told you about them, or maybe you had no idea who they were at all. It doesn't matter why now. I'm just glad you did. Thank you for allowing me to come into your living room, so to speak, and share my family with you. After all, my grandparents were just ordinary people with extraordinary jobs. Simply put, we were a multi-flavored handful of biscuits, traveling through life in the same basket.

Our family Christmas 2022

Photo by Dee Harris

We have our four Border Collies.

Photo by Dee Harris

We also have two Palominos, a pony, and a miniature donkey.

Yes, Roy and Dale were screen legends and bigger-than-life heroes. They impacted many lives and changed the social landscape. But they touched me in a very personal way, as only a grandparent can. So in my heart, they will always remain ... just Grandma and Grandpa.

To my family and friends, and new friends I have yet to meet, *Happy Trails!*

Until we meet again, Julie

Ingram Content Group UK Ltd.
Milton Keynes UK
UKHW022014030523
421159UK00015B/444